THE TAMIAMI TRAIL

A COLLECTION OF STORIES

by
Maria Stone

90th Anniversary Edition

ECity • Publishing

THE TAMIAMI TRAIL
A COLLECTION OF STORIES

© 1998, Maria Stone, original edition
© 2018, Marya Repko, copyright renewed with additional material
 All rights reserved.

set in Times New Roman, 10/12pt
printed & bound in the USA
Second Edition, First Printing, April 2018

cover photo courtesy Florida State Archives

ABOUT THE TYPE FACE
"Times New Roman" was designed in 1931 by English typographer Stanley Morrison (1889-1967) for the London newspaper *The Times*.

ISBN 978-0-9830425-6-3

ECITY • PUBLISHING

**P O Box 5033
Everglades City, FL, 34139
telephone (239) 695-2905**
www.ecity-publishing.com

Other books from this publisher:
 A Brief History of the Everglades City Area
 The Story of Everglades City; A History for Younger Readers
 Historia de Everglades City (Spanish translation by Gloria Gutiérrez)
 A Brief History of the Fakahatchee
 A Brief History of the Smallwood Store in Chokoloskee, Florida
 A Brief History of Sanibel Island
 The Story of Sanibel Island; A History for Younger Readers
 Angel of the Swamp; Deaconess Harriet Bedell in the Everglades
 Grandma of the Glades; A Brief Biography of Marjory Stoneman Douglas
 Memories from Hadlyme; A Personal History of the East Haddam, CT, Area
 Women in the Everglades; Pioneers and Early Environmentalists
 The Story of Barron Collier; A History for Younger Readers

PREFACE TO THE 2018 EDITION

As we celebrate the 90th Anniversary of the completion of the Tamiami Trail through the glades, it is particularly suitable that this book be republished with its "written oral history" of the people who lived and worked back in that formative era for Southwest Florida.

Author/publisher Maria Stone was a teacher in Immokalee with a love of local history. She interviewed dozens of old-timers to record their memories which she then transcribed into a series of books *(see the list on page 69)* – invaluable resources for other historians.

I am reprinting Maria's original 1998 book much as it was except for reformatting, adding photos and/or captions, and correcting a few typing mistakes.

My thanks to Lila Zuck, the literary curator of the late Maria Stone's work, for selecting me to republish this fascinating volume about our area history.

If you have comments or corrections or can add more to the story, please let me know.

Marya Repko
Everglades City, FL
mrepko@earthlink.net
April 2018

Note. The original cassette tapes of Maria's interviews have been donated to the Everglades Society for Historic Preservation and will be converted into computer files that can be saved on CDs. See www.evergladeshistorical.org for more information.

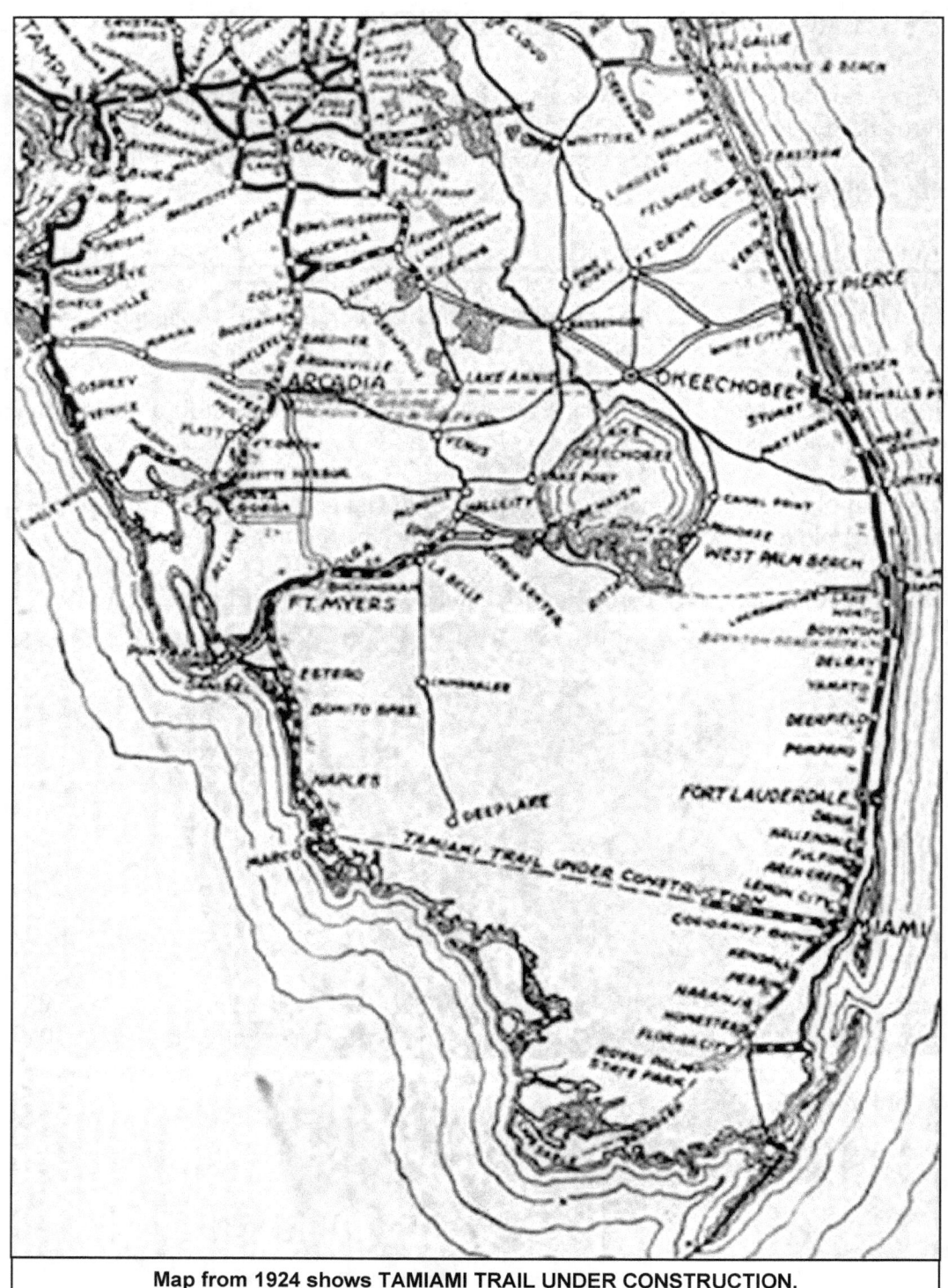

Map from 1924 shows TAMIAMI TRAIL UNDER CONSTRUCTION.

CONTENTS

Preface	1
Introduction to the Everglades	3
Maria Stone, *The Path Between Two Coasts*	5
Judy Sproul, *My Grandfather Barron Gift Collier*	9
Meece Ellis and Era Ellis, *Our Life Building and Living the Trail*	15
W.J. Rutledge, *The Dynamite Man*	21
Dinks Bogges, *I Was On Fire*	22
Alto and Hazel Griffin, *The "Tampa Kid" and Our Life on the Trail*	23
Colonel Frank F. Tenney, Jr, USAF, Ret. *Tamiami Trail History*	27
Lurleen Echols Chesser, *Living in the Laundry*	35
Harley Chesser, *Riding Night Patrol*	36
John Briggs, Sr., *Mr. Barron Collier's Chauffer*	37
L.L. Hampton, *The Man with a Plan*	40
Robert Bruce Warren, *Little Snake Hunter of the Everglades*	41
Lowell Goldie, *My Days on the Trail*	46
Ed Thompson, *Memories of the Trail*	47
Daryl Gay, *The Frog Hunter*	52
Keith King, *Indians at Monroe Station I Knew*	53
Lillian Larkins Weaver, *Our Life in Collier County, 1929-1934*	55
Lillian Larkins Weaver, *Postscript to Our Life in Collier County*	58
Further Reading	68
Books by Maria Stone	69
Time Line	70

Editor's Note: This preliminary page and all those that follow were included in Maria Stone's book. Some of the photos have been added in this edition.

THE TAMIAMI TRAIL

The Tamiami Trail includes a collection of personal memories of those connected with the building of the Tamiami Trail. This also is an in-depth look at this project by Colonel Frank F. Tenney, (USAF) Retired.

DEDICATION

This book is dedicated first of all to the catalyst of the Tamiami Trail, Barron G. Collier, Sr., Meece Ellis, W. J. Rutledge, "Doc" Johnston, the Seminole Indians, and many others who shared the daily drudgery of building the Tamiami Trail.

It is also dedicated to Colonel Frank F. Tenney, Jr., (USAF, retired), for his preservation of the factual and pictorial stories of the building of the Tamiami Trail. Collier County owes a great debt to Colonel Tenney for preserving his histories of Collier County. His tireless dedication has preserved many stories and pictures that would have been lost or discarded during these years of development. He has always graciously shared his files with those who desired to use the information. This author owes Colonel Tenney a great debt of gratitude for his unselfish sharing as she works toward her goal of preserving Collier County folk history.

It is also dedicated to an unnamed angel who made this book possible.

ACKNOWLEDGEMENTS

My deepest gratitude to the following people who contributed pictures and text.
- Colonel Frank J. Tenney, USAF, Ret.
- Collier County Historical Society
- Maureen Sullivan Hartung
- Eddie Hawkins
- Robert Bruce Warren
- Hazel & Alto Griffin
- Mildred Roberts Sherrod
- The Florida Department of Transportation
- Alice Darby
- Gerry Johnson, *Naples Daily News*
- Mr & Mrs. John Briggs, Sr.
- Peter Stone's Files

PREFACE

Some of the excerpts in this book have been taken from Folk Historian, Maria Stone's books, *Dwellers of the Sawgrass and Sand, Volumes I, II and III*. These tales were told to Mrs. Stone over a period of several years by the people who lived in the Everglades and witnessed its changing from swamp to the carving of a road linking Tampa to Miami on April 26, 1928.

The people who came for the building of the road through the Everglades were a hearty group. They suffered many adversities during the building of the Trail. Many stayed, some to run the way stations that Mr. Barron Collier established along the Trail. The Trail had its own patrol. The Southwest mounted Motorcycle patrolmen were issued scarlet tunics and black pants and wore Canadian Mountie style hats. Not having enough uniforms for the opening day ceremony, Mr. Collier dispatched his personal secretary, Florence Smith Thomason, to a costume house to get the needed uniforms. It was Mr. Collier's thought that these uniforms would add a lot of color to the parade and the opening ceremony.

The way stations were spaced approximately ten miles apart in order to accommodate the many motorists who came to view America's unique Everglades. It is a swamp combining both salt water and fresh water; a habitation for many forms of wild life as well as vegetation known and seen in no other part of the United States.

The building of the Trail through the Everglades has been likened to the building of the Panama Canal. The Trail joined the Gulf of Mexico with the Atlantic Ocean. It covers 110 miles, beginning from the city of Naples and ending on the outskirts of Miami. Some said that it could never be built. It was built through swamps infested with poisonous snakes, panthers and alligators. The builders fought raging wild fires, mosquitoes and swamp rot of the feet from having to stand and work in waist-deep water all day long. They also had to contend with the merciless sun as well as a hurricane in 1926 which brought a tidal wave in its wake that destroyed parts of the roadway and bridges that had just been built. New equipment was built to forge through the tangled mess that was the Everglades. But the men and women who forged ahead had grit and determination.

Barron Collier was a genius at invention. He ordered the construction of the first trailer that was used to house the men working on the Trail as well as bunkhouses and a mess area for feeding his men. He commissioned a huge dredging machine that moved tons of earth and paved the roadway. This walking dredge is on permanent display at the Collier-Seminole State Park on Highway 41 on the outskirts of the city of Naples. It was a noisy giant that ate up the muck and mud of the Everglades and smoothed the roadway as it slowly moved along.

The sheer logistics of building the Trail were staggering. Mr. Collier had to run boats from Fort Myers to Everglades to bring not only the food supplies but also the dynamite needed for blasting and thousands of gallons of gasoline daily. The boats ran from Fort Myers to Everglades and then by barge to the work sites. There were two warehouses set up, one in Carnestown and one in Port Dupont, the black settlement across the river, for holding dynamite, spare parts for the machinery and other supplies and materials needed by the men and the machines. A sawmill was built to furnish the needed lumber for the building of bridges.

Chief among Collier's selected workers was a man by the name of D. Graham Copeland, a brilliant engineer from South Carolina. Collier set up a construction company, and this firm under the guidance of D. Graham Copeland, built the Trail. Copeland is remembered as a fair man who took his challenge seriously. He had been charged with the duty of building a roadway from Royal Palm Hammock to the Dade County line. The Trail is 77 miles long in Collier County and was the most difficult segment to build of the total 275 miles from Tampa to Miami.

Another engineer charged with the building of the Trail was Robert Wilson who came to Naples in 1926. He and other workers wore long-sleeved shirts to deter mosquito bites, wide-brimmed hats to keep the sun off their faces and high boots for the long hours in the murky waters.

Maria Stone ~ THE TAMIAMI TRAIL

With the giant dredging machine working 18 hours a day, Copeland's people could dig a canal 24 feet wide and approximately 12 feet deep. Behind this giant machine workers laid lime rock a foot thick. Alongside, floating in the canals as they were built and filled with water were the boats and barges housing the men and some of their families as well as the mess halls where they were fed.

The huge dredging machine had no problem scooping the muck from the Everglades until they hit an almost impenetrable foe: lime rock. Dynamite was the only answer. It was said that the cost of dynamiting one mile through the Everglades was in excess of $20,000. Where machines and horses could not go the oxen could. It took two teams of oxen to haul the dynamite to the sites.

Everglades was just a spot on the map until the building of the Trail. It became a boomtown in the 1920s. Barron Collier built the Rod and Gun Club in Everglades City and it was the first county seat. He moored his yacht there. He realized the highway he had dreamed of when the official opening was held on April 26, 1928. Collier County became a reality also in 1923. Barron Collier was a man of foresight and many accomplishments. He died March 13, 1939.

The stories in this book encompass life at some of the way stations that Barron Collier built to service the motorists on the Tamiami Trail at its completion. They are told by many of the people who lived at the way stations Collier established. Among the workers on the Trail was Meece Ellis whose story is included in the following pages. He worked on the Trail for five years and then stayed with the Collier Company to maintain the expensive equipment. He is the man who operated the 20-ton walking dredge, and he is the man who moved the dredge from Royal Palm Hammock into its present location at the State Park. His story is in this book.

Another interesting story about the building of the Trail is by Mr. Keith King who operated the Monroe, Paolita and Glader Park Stations on the Trail during a 30-year period. While the trail was being constructed, oxen were used to haul dynamite to the dynamite crews. While on the Trail Mr. King acquired an ox yoke used by these animals that hauled dynamite. Mr. Duval Evans, a long-time friend of Mr. King's related to Maria Stone, the author of this book, that Mr. King wished to present the yoke to the Collier County Museum. Mr. and Mrs. Stone drove to Mr. King's home in Waverly, Illinois, to bring the yoke back to Naples. It is now on display at the museum. Mr. King daily befriended the Indians and the Miccosukee Tribe presented him with a plaque of appreciation signed by Billy Cypress, a Seminole Chief. His story is told in this book.

Mr. Alto Griffin's story appears in this book, also. He came to Ochopee and opened a garage in 1929 while working for the Gaunt family where he was charged with keeping the farm machinery running. He also had a wrecker and Hazel, his wife, remembered that he picked up wrecked cars daily. The Trail was a rough road built of shell materials. It was a good proving ground for tire manufacturers. The roadway itself was built with limerock boulders lining the road. This seemed to insure that cars hitting the rocks usually tipped over and went into the canals where more damage was done to their automobiles. Mr. Griffin assembled his wrecker from spare parts; unfortunately when retrieving a vehicle someone had to swim into the canal to hook the winch to the car. He saw many accidents and many deaths along the Trail. He left for private business after serving as the wrecker operator for over 12 years.

Before the work could begin the mammoth task of surveying for the Trail had to be done. R. E. "Doc" Johnson was 18 years old when he was hired on the survey team. "I was from Georgia and we had mosquitoes there, but they didn't compare to those in the Glades. These would pin you to the cheesecloth tent if you got against it in your sleep."

The man with the foresight for building the Trail was Captain Jaudon who envisioned around 1910 the great possibility of joining the east and west coasts of Florida by a loop road encircling the state. Captain Jaudon was a Miami tax assessor at the time when travel from Tampa to Miami had to be made by boat from Ft. Myers, around the Keys and up the coast to Miami, a trip encompassing weeks of sea travel.

Captain Jaudon envisioned a nearer and faster way to cover the miles. He had a dream that seemed impossible. He persuaded Lee and Dade Counties to begin the Trail project in 1915 and the road reached from Tampa to Fort Myers soon thereafter. The impossible dream became reality in 1923 when Barron Collier became the catalyst. There was no Collier County until 1923. Collier had purchased almost a million acres of land in southern Lee County. He promised the legislators that he would build the Trail if they would make a new county out of his land and name it Collier County. At his death, the Fort Myers News Press estimated his net worth as $17,000,000. He was known as a widely traveled, sophisticated man who considered his greatest accomplishment the building of the Tamiami Trail. With the opening of this roadway the Everglades became accessible to everyone.

INTRODUCTION TO THE EVERGLADES

The Everglades cover an area of approximately 928 square miles along the lower one-third of the state of Florida. The name Everglades is an Indian word meaning River of Grass. It is a place where salt and fresh water meet to create a unique Eco-system found no other place on our planet. It supports wild life as well as exotic vegetation. Many varieties of birds live within its confines, and the vegetation found here is like none other. The area abounds with alligators, snakes, aquatic animals and birds. A short stroll along one of the pull-offs along the Trail will insure you of seeing alligators living in the wilds within feet of where you stand. The sights, sounds and smells of the Everglades will live in your memory long after you depart.

The first inhabitants were tribes of indigenous people. When they came and where they came from has been lost in history. Archeology tells us thousands of years ago the aboriginal Indian tribes were here during the age of huge bison and tigers. The present day Seminoles and Miccosukees are now believed to be a blending of various Creek tribes from northern Florida and southern areas of Georgia and Alabama. The Native Americans played a part in the preservation of these wetlands. They lived with nature, killing only what they could eat.

They suffered during Seminole wars with the United States, especially during President Jackson's term. His fight to exterminate them from 1823 to 1859 proved more difficult than he imagined. The Indians survived by pushing far into the interior where they endured much hardship in the years following. They preserved their culture and today live in two worlds.

The three Seminole Wars in which the Seminole tribes were decimated, but in the end retained custody of their precious Everglades was a fight for their true heritage. They hold the distinction of never having signed a peace treaty with the United States.

With the incursion of the white man the Seminoles were pushed back farther into the Everglades. Today they live in several distinct areas of the Everglades, some on reservations, others as independent tribes who choose their homes either within or outside the limits of the reservations. We have them to thank for being the first preservers of this land we call Everglades.

The first white families to arrive in the Everglades included the Preston Sawyer family who came in 1870. (See *The Caxambas Kid* by Maria Stone.) The W. T. Collier family came to Marco in 1870 and W. D., the son of W.T., is known as the Father of Marco. Then came the Stevens and Barfield families as well as E. J. Watson who arrived in Chatham Bend around 1900. The Brown family of Immokalee, and the Bob Roberts family, also of Immokalee, came in 1800 on a cattle drive, and the Pettits who settled in Goodland also were among those first arrivals. Other families who arrived in the Chokoloskee area during this period were the Hamiltons, Browns, House and Santini. The Santini family became well known later for Flipper, the trained dolphin. Mr. Ted Smallwood established a trading post with the Indians in 1906 in Chokoloskee. It remains today, preserved for future generations. The Weeks brothers, Madison and John deserted the army during the War Between the States and came to live on Gordon Pass. Captain Charles Stewart came in 1900 at the behest of Mr. Haldeman to ferry people and goods by boat from the Tampa area to Ft. Myers and Naples.

With the settling of areas along the fringes of the Everglades during these early days, the land began to take on more importance for the people living here. During World War II servicemen came to be trained and then returned to live in this paradise when that war was over. It was during this time that the face of the area began to change, bringing more people, better roads and tourism. When Hurricane Donna came in 1960 it changed forever the face of the Everglades. It was the worse hurricane in modern recollection, and brought instant recognition to this little-known area. People from other areas of the United States began to take an interest in this place called the Everglades.

Marjory Stoneman Douglas, an activist in preserving the wetlands, gave talks and wrote books about the Everglades. She has been, and continues to be at the age of 106, one of the strongest proponents in seeing that the Everglades remain unchanged. Her many books speak of her desire to preserve the area, and she has been unflagging in her efforts to see that it retains its pristine beauty.

President Harry Truman dedicated the Everglades as a national park on December 6, 1947. Vice-President Gore was present at the fifty-year celebration in 1997. Since that time the area has captured the attention of many who have been instrumental in preserving the great swampland. It is the wish of the author that all who come to the Everglades enjoy it today and return in later years with friends and family and enjoy again the unchanged scenery and beauty which we native Floridians call the Everglades.

Without the building of the Tamiami Trail few of us would ever have the chance to experience the glory of the Everglades and its wildlife.

The building of the Trail changed the Indians' life style to some extent. Some stayed to live along the Trail. A few are there today. Many moved farther back or to reservations. O.B. Osceola and his parents, Cory and Juanita, lived near Ochopee and worked on the Jim Gaunt farm in Ochopee. Several Indians helped in planning the route and in surveying the Trail.

The Tamiami Trail opened a new frontier it is true but has no doubt brought development that has harmed the glory of the Everglades. We must all strive to preserve what is left of the Everglades.

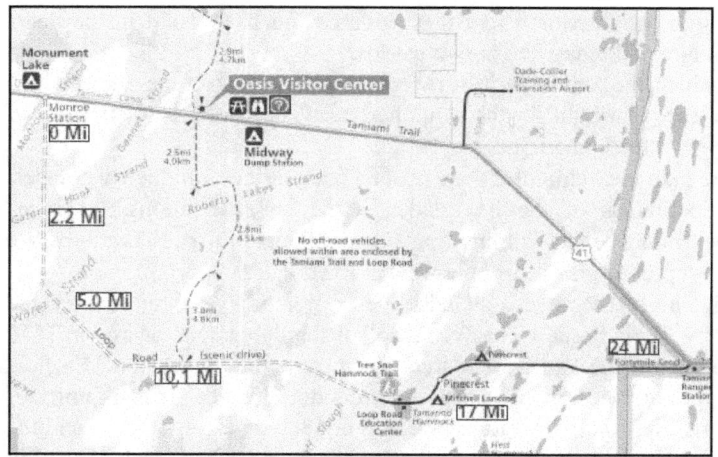

It was the dream of Capt. J.F. Jaudon, a Miami businessman, to complete the road between Tampa and Miami which went through his land in the Everglades. He started by building what is now called the "Loop Road" in Big Cypress National Preserve.

THE PATH BETWEEN TWO COASTS
The Tamiami Trail
by Maria Stone

Building the Tamiami Trail was a monumental challenge similar to the building of the Panama Canal, though in reverse. As you drive any part of the Tamiami Trail do you appreciate its magnificent history? Hazardous labor and perseverance made the dream a reality. This is the story of a miracle in the Everglades that many said could not happen.

Building the Trail was a matter of daily endurance for men, animals and machinery. The Tamiami Trail changed a two-day roundabout journey into less than a two-hour trip to Miami.

Who first dreamed the dream? It was a man as early as 1895 named Captain J. F. Jaudon. He settled in Miami and talked about his idea of a loop road someday encircling the state of Florida. In those very early days a person wishing to go to Miami from the lower West Coast would have to travel by train north and east to Jacksonville, then ride by train down the East Coast to Miami.

Captain Jaudon dreamed of this expansion happening during his lifetime. It was in 1914 and 1915 that he and his friends with Indian Guide Jack Tigertail surveyed the Everglades from the East Coast several times in canoes. Sometimes they walked the proposed Trail looking for the possibility of a right of way west through the Everglades from Miami. Captain Jaudon had planned to drain and sell land for farming and development. This he did when the Trail finally became passable. A journalist for the Miami Herald, William Stewart Hill supported the idea of a road connecting the two coasts of Florida. His articles helped enlist support for Captain Jaudon's dream.

Others on the West Coast became inspired. In 1915 Mr. Francis Perry of Ft. Myers, President of Chamber of Commerce traveled to the Tallahassee Legislature with Captain Jaudon to arouse interest in bringing the dream to life. Mr. Crayton of Naples and Mr. George Storter of Everglades also accompanied them.

The romantic name Tamiami Trail was coined by I. Dixie, President of Tampa Board of Trade and who was attending the highway commission meeting. Many names were suggested at that meeting. The Central Highway Commission had been formed in 1915, and the Trail proposed, but no name seemed to be appropriate until a combination of Tampa and Miami pleased those in attendance, especially since it was an age-old Indian Trail between Tampa and Miami.

There was some opposition to the Trail from various East Coast residents. "You will destroy Miami," they said. "It will flood the whole city," they predicted. At this point in the discussion World War I was declared and that halted the discussion of the project.

In the very early 1900s there came a dynamic man to the West Coast of Florida. His name was Barron Gift Collier, a financier and advertising executive from New York, but a native of Memphis, Tennessee. Mr. Barron Gift Collier would be the catalyst who provided the means, the ingenuity and ability to expedite the link between the east and west coasts. He was the missing link in Captain Jaudon's dream of a loop road around Florida through the strange and silent world of the Everglades, which was home to the Seminole Indians, snakes and alligators more than eight feet long. Mr. Collier had the vision to know that a highway through the wild Everglades would open a vast new frontier – namely the whole West Coast of Florida.

Until the birth of the Trail, this land was all part of Lee County. He deserves much praise for his efforts in establishing Collier County in 1923, and a new county seat in Everglades City, as well as opening the path between two coasts on April 26, 1928. Because of his efforts, the county bears his name. With his innate genius he was, indeed, the driving force that moved the indomitable project to fruition.

In 1923 when the idea of the new road was in its infancy, a group of twenty men made a treacherous and exhausting trip over the proposed route. This was done as a national publicity stunt across the Everglades because interest in the project was lagging. They were referred to as the "Trail Blazers." The Trail Blazers started in Ft. Myers on April 4, 1923. Mr. Ora Chapin was the promoter.

The Indian guide, Abe Lincoln, (Indian name Assumhachee) with Little Billie, led them through parts of the Indian canoe and oxen trails. These promoters were insistent that the Trail be built in Lee and Dade counties, excluding Monroe County. Ten Model-T cars and one heavy Elcar, an overland, began the journey. The Elcar bogged down, and when it was finally free of the muck, the owner returned with it to Ft. Myers. W. Stanley Hanson, Jr., was an agent for the Seminoles and spoke their language. Maurice Ayer was the only civil engineer along. Most of the men had not spent time in the woods. Only two knew the woods. They were Charles Hunt and Clark Taylor.

The first night some of the group slept in comfort at Everglades City and received a great send-off the following morning. Their next stop was Deep Lake to pick up part of their group who had spent the night there. After Deep Lake, travel was often at a standstill. For hours they hacked cypress to make way for the single line of struggling cars. From the Cypress swamps they sank in black muck, only to plunge into marl, followed by dusty prairies and blistering sun overhead. Their food supply was dwindling as well as their water supply. They ate cattail roots and swamp cabbage. When Indian, Little Billie went hunting for deer meat he failed to return. During the remainder of the 23 days, Abe Lincoln cut hollow reeds for them to sip water through the holes in the bedrock.

Mr. Cyril Sawcross became the cook for each night when they camped. Sometimes he had to improvise with their scarce rations. What was to be a three-day trip had turned into a 23-day trip. Milton Thompson was 15 years old and the youngest of the Trail Blazers. He was taken along as a mechanic. Most of this material is from his diary, courtesy of Mary Nan Ellis, his daughter. The outside world had decided that the Trail Blazers were hopelessly lost, when a plane from Miami spotted them and dropped supplies. At that point they knew they could finish the course.

The bedraggled group reached Canal Grade, which was a dredged rock bed built on Australian pine roots, and arrived in Miami to the relief of many. The Model-Ts were missing fenders, headlights, running boards, and any part that happened to catch on a cypress stump. Henry Ford had the Miami Ford dealer completely recondition their cars before they headed for home. They had proved that a path between two coasts made building a road possible.

Now came the days, months and years of organizing equipment and manpower, and finances to tackle the monumental task of a road across this treacherous and mysterious wilderness. Apparently Mr. Collier was a man who could visualize the end result before the beginning. When it all began an old timer, "Doc" Johnson came from Georgia in 1926. He was recruited at the age of 18. Doc was one of the groups of advance surveyors on the right of way. A number of Indians were included. Many times they stood in water from knee deep to waist deep. He also ran the dragline later to set fill on the bedrock. The drillers had a difficult job boring holes under the water and also hard rock limestone to set dynamite. Holes were placed six feet apart and fourteen feet deep. Blasting began at 7:30 A.M. each morning.

Mr. W. J. Rutledge was the man in charge of dynamiting. It was hauled in carts drawn by a team of oxen. Several teams had to be available as those who stood too many days in water developed foot rot. When the carts and oxen stuck fast in the muck, men carried dynamite to the site. The mosquitoes swarmed in black clouds day and night. It was reported that panthers attacked the camp from time to time, drawn by the odor of fresh meat.

One night some men in camp felt safe standing in neck deep water until the panthers moved off. Some workers were convicts and escapes happened, but often the world out there was harsher than confined life on the Trail. These cases caused manhunts, but in spite of that, the Trail inched on one half mile a month. Barron Collier is quoted as saying, "We who built this Trail literally blasted our way through solid rock to do it."

Three million sticks of dynamite were used. That is reported to be enough to reach from Florida to California. For a time the progress was lagging. William S. McAdoo, former Secretary of the Treasury, suggested that the workers be given a bonus. After that progress moved forward more rapidly. The whole workforce experienced the 1926 hurricane and floods from the usual summer rains as well. Even a short drought worked a hardship, coupled with the ever-present deer flies, sand fleas and gnats.

Meece Ellis, Doc Johnson and W. J. Rutledge, all three, praise Mr. Collier for the way he provided food and care for the people who worked on the Trail. He had the respect and loyalty of the Trail builders.

In 1922 Mr. Meece Ellis began running the walking dredge that built the roadbed. He ran the noisy monster for long hours for six years. At present the walking dredge is on display in Seminole State Park.

It took a host of crews to provide for the sparse sleeping comforts: food, water and supplies for the road crews. At the onset Mr. Collier hired D. Graham Copeland as Chief Engineer. Workers were recruited from Alabama and Georgia. There were two boats to meet buses of recruits. Mr. Collier had three crews: one on the job, one leaving on the boat and one on the way to the job. The workers were paid $.20 an hour. It is said the Trail cost about $25,000 per mile. In this day and time the Trail would probably not be built because of the damage the construction would cause to the environment.

April 26, 1928 was a glorious day of celebration. A cavalcade of five hundred cars formed in Tampa. Governor Martin and Barron Gift Collier led the motorcade as it traveled south all the way to Everglades City. Many of the Trail Blazers, dignitaries and supporters rode in the motorcade. They arrived for a gala celebration in Everglades City where Josie Billie and others waited. Later in the afternoon the motorcade reached the Archway which marked the boundary between Collier County and Dade County.

The motorcade from the west met the motorcade from the east and moved on to Miami where another celebration was awaiting their arrival. In a sense it resembled the connecting of the Atlantic and Pacific Oceans when the Panama Canal was completed. The Tamiami Trail in a sense connected the Atlantic coast with the Gulf coast. The Panama Canal was referred to as the path between the seas. The Trail could be referred to as the path between two coasts.

The impossible had been done. A solid, durable road now crossed the once impenetrable untamed land. Though it was rather crude, if compared to roads built much later, it is a miracle. It is a monument to a great visionary, Barron Gift Collier. He has made his family proud.

On some occasion Mr. Barron Collier had seen the Royal Canadian Northwest Mounted Police perform in Madison Square Garden. This inspired him to establish the Southwest Mounted Police to patrol the newly opened Trail. Special uniforms and flags were designed for the patrolmen on motorcycles. They were to provide first aid and minor repairs for travelers. Way stations were built every ten to twenty miles along the new road. These were operated by husband and wife teams who lived at each station. They sold gas, cold drinks and sandwiches. They allowed hunters and fishermen to park their buggies and boats on the property. These patrolmen and the people at the way stations did a great service for those traveling through such remote country. Wild life was abundant. Cars were often damaged by alligators sprawled on the warm road. Many Trail tenders can tell tall tales about life along the Tamiami Trail.

Some Indians chose to live along the Trail and sell their goods. A few of them worked at the way stations. The names of the stations were Belle Meade, Royal Palm Hammock, Weaver's Camp, Turner River, Monroe Station and Paolita. There were also the villages of Ochopee and Carnestown. Refer to the book Ochopee, the Smallest Post Office.

In these modern times people speed along the Trail often missing the beauty of its wildness. Most are unaware of the toil, sweat and tears, and the many lives spent building the road they cruise along. The Everglades is still a strange and silent world, unique in the world. May the secrets it holds remain forever preserved. May the Tamiami Trail and its sawgrass world be preserved for the future. We must save the past for the future.

This is a short list of Barron Gift Collier's achievements in Florida in connection with and besides building of the Tamiami Trail.

He established Inter-County Telephone & Telegraph Company and the *Collier County News*. He built the county seat and Courthouse in Everglades City and opened the Bank of Everglades. He extended the Atlantic Coast Line Railway and started the Trailway Bus Line. He acquired a large fleet of steamers to carry freight and passengers.

He did not destroy the lifestyle of the Indians. He respected them. He allowed them the freedom to hunt and fish at will. They were allowed to carry on tribal rites and move camps as they pleased. They were free to cut any materials needed with no restrictions. When the Trail was open and the Trailway Bus line was established, the Indians were allowed to ride free. They could flag it anywhere they wished and get off anywhere they wished.

Barron Gift Collier was a friend to the Indian and non-Indian alike.

Barron Gift Collier was born in 1873 in Memphis and soon became a wealthy leader in streetcar advertising. In 1907 he married local gal Juliet Carnes and they had three sons: Barron, Jr., Sam, and Miles (seen above with D. Graham Copeland). Collier died in 1939 after visiting his beloved Useppa Island. His wife Juliet died in 1971 in New York.

MY GRANDFATHER BARRON GIFT COLLIER
Judy Sproul

My real name is Juliet, named after both my grandmothers – my grandmother on my father's side and my grandmother on my mother's side. Actually, my Grandmother Collier did not know my Grandmother May, but she knew my Grandfather May. Barron, Sr., and my Grandfather May knew each other in New York. My Grandfather May was a senior partner in Price Waterhouse. They were nice friends and respected each other, though were not terribly close.

My oldest daughter is named Katherine Gordon after my grandmother's sister. My middle daughter is Juliet after my grandmothers. My name was always switched to Judy as a nickname, and I always said I regretted it, as I always loved the name Juliet, so we tried to straighten it out with my middle daughter's name.

The youngest daughter is Jennifer. The three girls are 20, 22 and 28. They were born in Greenwich. I met my husband on a blind date in Connecticut visiting my cousin. He lived in New York at that time. I had just finished two years of college and was transferring down to Florida to spend more time with my family. I met my husband and changed my plans, and went back to New York.

I lived in New York ten months and married him. Actually, he and my grandmother became quite great friends. She was living in New York at that time.

My mother was Barbara May. She and my father met in New York. Actually, she had gone out with my father's younger brother, Sam. They were just friends. My father, Barron Collier, Jr., had been on a long, committed relationship about six years. I guess my mother caught his eye, and they began to see each other after he broke up with the other lady.

The grandparents met in Memphis. Grandmother was born and brought up in Memphis. Barron, Jr., was, also. Grandmother was from a well-to-do family. Grandfather went out and went to work very hard. He got involved in advertising in New York. He was also involved in the street lighting. He did quite well financially, and came back and asked Juliet to marry him.

Barron, Sr., was from Memphis too. They were married, and my father, Barron, Jr., was born in Memphis. You know, I can relate to this. When I got to know my Grandmother Juliet, Barron, Sr., had been dead quite a while. My husband had been gone quite a while, too. We tended to live in the present and not always in the past. We didn't talk all that much about the past.

My grandmother was very much of an influence on me, particularly. My parents were separated when I was about 12 years old. I felt fat and unattractive, and alone, as happens at that age. Grandmother took me under her wing. She was a lovely, gracious, charming woman. They almost don't make them like that anymore. She was very, very special.

I had one sister, Barbara, named after our mother. Grandmother was very interested in people. She loved dogs, too. She always had dogs. She did beautiful needlepoint, and loved to travel. She had a great friend who was also from Memphis, who was Mrs. Crump. She had also lost her husband. They traveled together a great deal. They went to Europe a lot. They took me to Hong Kong when I was 16.

They were of different personalities. My grandmother was a sort of private person. She didn't display affection openly, but was a very warm person. Mrs. Crump was very bubbly and chit-chatty. When we went shopping Mrs. Crump would say, "Bring all the things out to show me. Do you want this? Do you want this?" When my grandmother bought something, it was done very quietly and put away. She'd use it as a gift at Christmas or such an occasion.

It was great fun traveling with them. They complemented each other's beautiful personalities. They enjoyed life very much.

At that time widows – especially prominent widows – didn't remarry. I think it was too bad my grandmother didn't. She did have a beau. He took her to the opera and the theater. She was very much interested in those. She loved to have people in her home. She liked to have dinner parties. In the 1950s she bought a home in Palm Beach. My father, Barron, Jr., was living at that time. Before that she had her own apartment in Boca Grande Hotel on Boca Grande Island. It was at the very end, toward the golf course. It was a very nice, large apartment, with three or four bedrooms. I remember going to visit her there. It was during the war years. My father was in the Corps of Engineers. My mother would take us there, and we would live in one of the little cottages. We spent three or four winters down there. I remember being on the beach at Boca Grande.

We went through bankruptcy after he died. We were left well off, but weren't involved in a lot of business ventures then. We had the land in Florida, but it wasn't worth much then.

Grandfather Barron, Sr., had lived a very nice lifestyle for years. They had a home in Germany and in Pocono Hills in New York State. The three brothers still raced. They had a dirt track up there. Barron, Jr., Sam, and Miles used to race cars. Barron, Jr., was the oldest son. Then Sam, then Miles. When Barron, Sr., bought the castle in Germany he sent Florence Thompson, a secretary, to take inventory and catalog all the contents.

Back to my grandmother – I certainly appreciated getting to be special friends with my grandmother. Oftentimes, one doesn't get to be friends with grandparents. She used to call me up and say, "Judy, what are you doing?" I'd maybe say, "I'm making curtains." I was living a very different type of life than she did when she was my age. She appreciated the fact that I did certain things. Of course, when I married and lived in New York, we got to see a lot of her. She had a lovely apartment overlooking Central Park. We often had dinner with her. She died in 1971 in New York. She had cancer. She hated the hospital. She had a marvelous doctor for years. He used to come to the house. After her last, short stint in the hospital he said, "We will make you comfortable at home." She died peacefully in her New York apartment. Up until the very end she was spry and very much "the lady."

My husband and I, the oldest daughter, and the middle one who was two years old, went in for Christmas. She wasn't strong at all, but the table was beautifully set with finger bowls – everything. We had Christmas lunch. She sat with us for 15 minutes – just the regal lady that she was. That was the last time I saw her. She died within a week. She used to love to have us come in. I used to pick up my oldest daughter even when she was in kindergarten and drive in from Greenwich – about an hour's drive. We'd sit in her library. I'd have a cocktail. My daughter would have her cookies and milk. We would have a nice chat for maybe an hour and a half, then we would drive back home. We used to do this about every other week.

Clark Ansley worked with my grandfather when he brought Snooky over from Germany to the Rod and Gun Club. I go to meetings and there are pictures of my grandmother and grandfather staring down at me. It is fun. It really is.

My grandfather came to Florida in 1911 and bought Useppa Island. He really did love Useppa. That was a special place. I don't think my grandmother was quite as enthusiastic, at first. It was isolated, and she wasn't used to that type of life. Later on there were stories about when family friends came down to fish here was this lady making everyone pancakes when she had servants. She was a southern-lady hostess. My parents are dead; both my grandparents are dead.

My daughters are very interested in the link to the past, but it's not possible for them to go to grandparents and say, "What was going on?" My father was very interested in genealogy. He said he could trace our family back to the first baby born in Virginia who was Virginia Dare.

My father, Barron, Jr., loved history. We couldn't even buy him a history book he didn't already have. He was especially involved in the Civil War. He and his brothers had their own toy soldiers. Barron, Jr., and Sam had their own armies. When we lived in Connecticut our house had a third floor that the kids used as a playroom. Certain times of the year they would get together and do wars. They converted the little guns that could be bought at Woolworth's, so they would shoot little nails. There were certain types of tanks. My brother still has my father's whole collection. My father remarried. Margarite had four children. They had Barry between them. Barron Collier here in Naples is my nephew.

Maria Stone ~ THE TAMIAMI TRAIL

I remember we came to Florida to visit at Useppa. We moved to Florida in 1950. Sam was killed in the car wreck in Watkins Glen, New York.

My father was the financial advisor. Sam and Miles were working down here in Florida. When Sam was killed we moved to the East Coast of Florida because my mother wanted a little more culture than was available here. We came over to fish at Boca Grande and spend time in Useppa. I knew both places as a child. In fact, when I went back two years ago there is still the guest register with my name in a sprawling, child-like manner. That was fun.

We used to spend time sun fishing off Useppa Beach. We used to go tarpon fishing. I have an Isaac Walton button on my charm bracelet that I got for catching a tarpon weighing 100 pounds. That was caught in Boca Grande Pass. My father, friends, niece, and I would get up at 4:00 A.M. and go fishing. We would come in at 10:00 or 11:00, nap, and go back out, then back out until late at night. That was fun.

When I was 14 my father would bring me over. We'd drive to the ranch, the Everglades and to Naples. This was in the 1950s. It was a little different than it is now. I like it the way it is today. It hasn't been bad the way it has developed.

I moved here over 18 years ago. This is my permanent home. Everything has to change and grow or else it becomes absolutely stagnant. I don't see a huge population explosion like the East Coast. I think the development will continue, but more slowly, maybe on a more tasteful scale. The environmental demands make it necessary. You cannot do things today that you did 20 years ago. It is good in a way, but it is difficult on the developer – but that makes them do a good job.

In the old days when you had mangroves in the way someone would get a backhoe and the mangrove would disappear. Today there is a much better understanding of the whole environmental process.

In the project that I'm doing we are going in and we are restoring wetlands. There are wetlands that have been overtaken by the pepper hedge and the melaleuka. They basically aren't wetlands anymore. We are going back in there and tearing those exotics out and reworking it into a wetland and leaving the cypress, so where all those undesirable pepper hedge and melaleuka were there will be a nice bird sanctuary.

What people don't realize is that those exotics are damaging to Florida. They are destructive. The amount of water an Australian pine takes up is massive. I think there are some good things happening in this project, and I am enjoying it. I just hope it doesn't get too much more complicated. It is so expensive from the financial standpoint. The amount of time and energy that has to be invested before ground can be broken is very high. Not many can afford it. This excludes the small developer, which is too bad. It's excluding a person who would start off in a small, entrepreneur way and grow. I don't see that happening today because of all the rules and regulations that are political, environmental and other such things. The Tamiami Trail couldn't be built today.

It was funny when you did the dedication of the signs for the Tamiami Trail that day at the Park and that marvelous man, the dynamiter, W. J. Rutledge, talked about how it was done when the Trail was built. Now the way we have to get all these permits and can only do so much at a time, the Trail could not be built today. It rather spoils the entrepreneurship of a project.

This project in Grey Oaks – it has a very nice lake on it that is quite deep which we are going to call Deep Lake. Deep Lake was the name of the very first piece of property that Barron, Sr., ever bought in Collier County. There was a citrus grove there. Someone wanted me to use that as the name for the project. I didn't think it appropriate for the entire project, but I think it's very appropriate for the lake. It is the Gites' pit that was used as an alternate water supply for the City of Naples for many years. It has good, clean water and fish in it. This project is basically Golden Gate Parkway and Airport Road. It corners there. It has 1,600 acres. It's a challenge. I think we are doing something very nice there.

One man who used to come to Boca Grande and Useppa was Mr. Buckner, a longtime friend of my Collier grandparents. I came across a picture the other day of my grandmother in a very elegant, long velveteen dress being escorted by Mr. Buckner in a top hat, white tie, and tails. Even after my grandfather died, Mr. Buckner visited my grandmother in Palm Beach. Dorothy Lamour came to visit us once. I remember the stories of her running around the beach barefoot. She let her hair down. She loved Useppa. When I was a child the only way to get to Boca Grande was by boat. You had to go to Bookelia and get in a boat, then, if you were going to Useppa, you had to get an another boat. It was a real special trip. My father used to have a lot of his army buddies on General MacArthur's staff down to go tarpon fishing in the full moon of May or the full moon of June. My grandmother was a gracious, southern lady, the kind Barron, Sr., needed for his style of life. She went along with almost anything he cared about. She could do almost anything. On our Hong Kong trip I locked my key and my passport in my trunk. She came up to my cabin with a screwdriver. With perspiration dripping off her forehead, she worked to get my trunk open. She was a neat lady, and very down to earth. I think she cared very deeply for Barron, Sr.

She was very proud of all her three sons. There was a picture of the three sons that used to hang in her entranceway. None of the boys liked it – neither Barron, nor Sam, nor Miles liked it. They thought they were sort of sissified in riding clothes. She'd keep saying to my father, "Now don't you want this picture? He'd say gruffly, "I don't want anything to do with that picture." I said, "I would love to have that picture." I didn't particularly care for it either, but she thought that it was great that someone wanted it. It was huge. It took up the entire wall. After she died I got some of her furniture, and out came that picture eight feet high. Her apartment had high ceilings to accommodate it. Sam died in a car accident in 1950, and two years later, in 1952, Miles, Sr. died of bulbar polio. It happened quickly. My father had tuberculosis, but he recovered.

I think Barron, Sr. was a man who liked challenges. He had a great imagination, and a great deal of energy. I guess I'd say he had great vision. He invented the white line that is in the middle and sides of our highways. He was Assistant Police Commissioner in New York when I was a teenager. I loved to tell my friends that. To me that was important – not that he bought land in Florida, but that he invented that white line on the roads. I don't know if he was interested in cars, but he must have been because all three boys were fascinated with cars.

I think there was something about Florida that he fell in love with. He didn't see it as a wilderness. I think he just looked at Florida for what it was. Maybe that's the way I feel, too. It seemed natural for him to be here. I know that here is where he felt most at home in his later years. He spent a lot of time in Useppa.

Preston Tuttle was the manager. Preston was nicknamed "G" for Giraffe because he had a long neck. He said, "You all are good friends and work well."

Jim said: "You all are good friends and work well."

I have a hard time going to Boca Grande. It's different. You can't always recreate the past. I think I'll just keep the special memory. Actually I'd be interested in seeing what Boca Grande is today, not for what it meant for me then. I think there were several men of the same vintage who had a great influence on Florida. Today I don't think one person can do something like they did. Florida was virgin territory.

When my grandfather came to Florida it was like going out west. It was virgin territory, basically. There was land to be claimed. You could buy it through the railroad or through various other ways. You could use your imagination. If you were living in more populated areas, things had already been done to develop the area. This was new country, and you could let your imagination go. That's why so many awesome things did happen. Who would ever think of building a bridge all the way to the Keys and connecting all those islands? That's amazing. There are a lot of very interesting things that happened in Florida because of imaginative, far-seeing persons.

My grandfather had more influence on the West Side of Florida than anyone. I think Barron, Sr. not only had a vision, but he tended to go after it. He made it come true. He was a strong person. I don't know this for sure, but I don't think he took "no" easily. He was very much goal-oriented. He came from not much, and he made a great deal of money. He was a self-made man, completely. Now my grandmother came from a well-to-do family. Part of the motivation was that he wanted to marry my grandmother, and he needed status to start courting her. He didn't have it when he first met her. He was told by my grandmother's father he couldn't marry my grandmother until he had $1 million, or some certain figure. That's absolutely what did it. He went after what he wanted, and he was going to get it. This determination is why he got Collier County named after him. He said, "If I finish Tamiami Trail, will you name the county after me?" They said, "Yes," so he did the Tamiami Trail.

My grandmother was a lovely, southern lady from Memphis. She always wore hats. I remember going to stores with her in New York when I was a teenager. I'd try on all of her hats. I am fortunate to have known my grandparents who were outstanding people as well as pioneers in Florida.

photo courtesy Florida State Archives

Meece Ellis operated the huge dredge during the building of the Tamiami Trail, digging up soil to created a roadbed. When the Trail was completed, he and his wife Era moved to Royal Palm Hammock where the road to Marco Island (CR-92) meets the Trail. They opened a tourist court for visiting anglers and built a restaurant on the corner. The original Patrol Station, the last one standing, still exists behind the modern gas station. Meece restored the dredge which can be seen in nearby Collier Seminole State Park.
See photos on previous page.

OUR LIFE BUILDING AND LIVING ON THE TRAIL
Meece and Era Ellis

My father was Robert Chappel Ellis. My mother was Lilly Belle Floyd before she married my father. I was born in 1903. I had four brothers and sisters. I was the first child. There was Floyd, Robert, Allen and Daisy Bell.

My father bought land on the Trail which is right where a trailer park (Meadow Circle) is at Gladiolis Boulevard turn off. My father raised vegetables.

I was seventeen, and I worked on the truck farm. In those early days of Ft. Myers there were still hitching posts for the horses in front of the stores. There were dirt roads and we paved with oyster shells. There wasn't much town.

I come to Collier County in early 1922. I was eighteen. I come with the first dredge that Mr. Collier bought to build the Tamiami Trail. I had never had any experience on a dredge. We rebuilt the dredge on the banks of the Allen River in Everglades. We dug the canal for the roadbed from Everglades out to Carnestown. From there we headed west to Royal Palm Hammock.

When we got to Carnestown Mr. Collier bought two Bay City dredges and they started east to Miami. I worked on a one-yard Marion floatin' dredge, too. It was on a steel barge sixteen feet wide and fifty feet long. It had a one cubic yard scoop bucket on it. That dredge had to have water to float. We had to dig the canal so deep at Royal Palm Hammock for it to float. That was as far as we got with a floating dredge. At that time there was a company building a roadbed from Ft. Myers to Marco. When they got to the Imperial River in Bonita Springs they found out they could work so much faster with a dragline. They left this Bay City dredge on the banks of the Imperial River right below Everglades Wonder Gardens. The Colliers bought this dredge. I went up there with two big barges and a towboat. We dismantled this dredge and loaded it on those barges. We brought this dredge around to Marco and unloaded it where the old ferryboat landing was. There is a bridge there now. We loaded that dismantled dredge on big trailers and we towed it around to Royal Palm Hammock.

We used the old road built in 1915 that went from Naples almost to Marco and then turned off and went around to Royal Palm Hammock. We assembled that dredge at Black Water River at the end where we had finished with the Marion dredge. We built the road west from Royal Palm Hammock up to Belle Meade. That is where #951 crosses the Trail now. We dismantled the dredge at that time and brought it back to the Monroe Station on the Tamiami Trail. The Loop Road had never been completed all around to the Trail. We finished that Loop Road which was four and six tenths miles to the Trail.

We then dismantled the dredge and brought it back to Royal Palm Hammock, put it back together, dug the canal and made the roadbed down about five miles going to Goodland.

We got into a lot of little creeks and stuff and couldn't use the walking dredge. We then brought it back to Royal Palm Hammock. We left it there right close to the road. Nobody knew anything about a park then, you see. They told me to put that dredge just as close to the road as I could so the next time we needed it we could get at it to haul it off.

Well, in 1937 Era and I went to live at Royal Palm Hammock Station. The first thing I had to do was move that dredge back off the road. The old original filling station then was on the west side of the Marco Canal. We wanted to move the filling station to the east side of the canal. I jacked up the dredge and had some house movers put dollies under it and move it back out of the way.

In 1946 or '48 when the park was established they wanted the dredge in the park. Well, it was up to me to move it again over into the park and there it sits right now. I moved that dredge four or five times.

When Mr. Collier bought the first two Bay City dredges the factory sent a man down there. My superintendent had me go out where he was and he showed me how to dismantle and put that dredge back together. I worked for the Colliers from 1922 to 1938.

Era said: My father, George Womble, had a farm right below us on the Tamiami Trail. He had four daughters. I'll name my sisters. The first one was Minnie Lee, I'm Era that's me, I was next, then came Opal and then Jimmy Kate.

Meese said: I met Era picking peppers.

Era spoke up: He said he liked the way I worked. My mother, Mae Womble wouldn't let me go on a date without my sister as a chaperone, and she was only fourteen. She liked to go because Meece would buy her a coke. We were married in 1928, the year the Trail was finished.

Meece explained: The Colliers had a lot of equipment left like those big dredges, etc. The depression was coming on, too. They had one big dragline and I operated it in Naples and around the county building several roads. They had one big dredge out on Immokalee Road right north where number I75 crosses number 29. They had $250,000 insurance on that dredge. The policy called for a man on that dredge all the time. I was the only man that knew how to operate it. There were two big steam boilers on there that had to be fired up once a month. I had to run the machinery even though it was just setting there. It was a big dredge that had living quarters on it for twenty-four people. It was a three-yard dredge. Era and I lived out there on that dredge from 1928 to 1934. There was so much work to do in Everglades City that I was called there. We worked in Everglades from 1934 to 1937. It was then as I said, we moved out to Royal Palm Hammock to take over that way station on the Trail.

The original station was 12 feet wide and 24 feet long and was two stories. When we moved the filling station we put a room on the front and had a small restaurant in front. We built four log cabins for rental. We finally built the building that's on the corner there now, the Swamp Buggy Grill Museum.

Back to building the Trail – Audrey Fredrick, whose wife was a teacher in Naples, was the surveyor at that time for the Colliers. Mr. Collier arranged everything. In 1923 this became Collier County and ceased to be part of Lee County. "Aud" Fredrick worked from Belle Meade east, all the way to the Forty-Mile Bend. Most of the labor came from South Georgia. Those boys off the farm up there, $1.50 a day at that time, was all they could make.

When they came to work on the Trial they got $60 a month and board. That was good money for a laborer at that time. They were the most dependable help we had. The only Indians we had did some right of way work. They were Billy Osceola, Abraham Lincoln, Jose Billie, Boy Jim and Charley Jumper. Charley was blind.

At Royal Palm Hammock Charley used to get out on the road with a walking stick. He walked along the side of the road. When he heard a car coming he would get off. A lot of people knew him and they would stop and pick him up. He would be going down to the Indian Camp at Big Cypress Bend. He visited back and forth. That is about 7 ½ miles, but he could walk it as blind as a bat.

Charley Tommie was an old Indian. He came from the Everglades. He drowned in the canal there. They had been to Chokoloskee when that happened.

The Georgia boys worked on the dredge and the dynamite drilling crew and what not. W. J. was the dynamite man. I've known W. J. Rutledge about all his life. Most of the work on the Trail to Royal Palm Hammock and Belle Meade had two ten-hour shifts. The dredges going east from Carnestown was working in solid rock all the time, all the way to Forty Mile Bend. If one shift did 80 feet that was all they could do in four hours. We started off with two dredges but we finally wound up with three. I was the first dredge man they had down there. I knew how to work all the dredges. If an operator got sick or quit I could fill in and replace him on any dredge.

The mosquitoes were terrible. We didn't have any repellent like we have today. We had citronella. We used B-Brand insect powder. The company bought that by the barrels. We would take a handful and put in on a paper sack and set the sack afire. The powder would burn slowly for two or three hours. It would run the mosquitoes off, but it put your eyes out. I tell you that. We did that on the dredge and in the bunkhouses, too. We had mosquito bars where we slept.

We had a few accidents, of course, when you have about fifty men working. One was when dynamite went off prematurely. It shook four men up but didn't kill them. The only fatality we had was on this Bay City dredge. When we were digging the Trail down to Marco Pass one man fell off the point of the boom. He fell into the bucket and split his head wide open. He was on Earl Ivey's shift.

At night a lot of time we'd use this old black mangrove and make a smudge pot in a ten-gallon bucket. That helped some. We would put a towel around our necks and around our heads and put our hats on. We would sleep with black gloves on, too because of mosquitoes.

On the dredge there was an operator and an oiler. He kept everything greased. The noise on that dredge was pretty bad, about like an airboat. The gasoline motor was right back of the operator. It was noisy. The cables running clank, clank all day and night made a lot of noise. When you are young you can take that.

The heat was bad in the summer. Most of the boys were used to the heat in Florida and Georgia. I'd say the biggest problem we had wasn't snakes but foot rot. Most of the time we were in the water. Even operators had to walk back and forth. The whole country was under water for a greater part of the year, you know. We would get what we called "Muck Poison" in our feet. Our shoes would get full of water and sand would get in there, too, and we were walking around irritating our feet, especially the boys that worked on the dynamite crew. They were in the water all the time.

When our feet got poisoned we had to go to the clinic in Everglades. They would give us this medicine to use and we would sit out in the open air with our feet in the sun to kill the poison. It took about two weeks to kill the poison. We lost a lot of hours on account of that. We had a lot of snakes and alligators everyday and night. A snake can't stand the heavy vibration that the dredges made, so that helped us some.

As I look back on this experience I'd like to live it over again.

Era said: He loved every minute of it because he was out in the woods.

Yes I did, said Meece. I like to hunt and fish. From the time we started that canal out of Everglades the snook followed those dredges right on out for the twenty miles. The canal would be full back behind us for two or three hundred yards. We didn't know how to cook snook those days. They were called soap fish. People didn't know to skin them at first. They scaled them. That skin is where the soap taste comes from.

I got paid $150 a month and board. The biggest problem we had to start off with was getting fresh red meat. All our provisions came from Fort Myers around by boat on the outside to Indian Key and up the channel to Everglades. In 1922 there was only ice and no electric refrigeration. The meat would be shipped by boat from Ft. Myers or Tampa to Everglades. It was then put on a run boat, which carried it out on the job. We seldom got a good piece of meat to eat. If it hadn't been for the venison and turkeys for about the first two years we would have been in trouble.

The Indians killed a good bit of it for us. They would bring game up there and we would buy a hen turkey for $.50 or a gobbler for $.75. We paid five or six dollars for a big deer. The woods was full of wild hogs at that time. The boys who worked on the dredges went huntin' on their time off to get us fresh meat, too. I used to kill three or four deer a week, and it took every bit of it. With that many men in a camp several deer didn't last long.

We had cured meat like ham, bacon and sausage, but we needed fresh meat. We had the best cooks you ever saw. We had one cook from Rosehill, South Carolina. She was Mrs. Ellis, but no kin to me. Her husband was a dredge operator. All of our cookhouses was on barges in the Canal. They had big wood-burning stoves and big, long tables in them. They were carried right along behind the dredge within one hundred yards of the dredge all the time. The cook lived in a barge behind the kitchen barge. We had gangplanks to walk to these barges. She cooked black-eyed peas, beans, rice, and grits. We had all the pie in the world.

Mrs. Fred Diden was the cook that cooked one shift. Her husband was a dredge operator, too. We had six big bunkhouses mounted on wheels. Each one would sleep twelve people to the house. They were towed right up behind the dredges all the time. As the dredge worked we threw the spoil rock back out on the road. We had a machine that leveled it off, but it was pretty rough still.

The first trailer houses in the United States were these cook houses and bunkhouses. They were built in Everglades City. Sometimes the dredges would be a quarter of a mile ahead of the sleeping quarters, but those boys could take the noise and sleep. We did this work from 1922 to 1928. The big problem sleeping was this, men would leave and would come back. Most men that came back had a little old pasteboard suitcase. Lots of them brought in bedbugs in those suitcases. Bedbugs were a real problem in the bunkhouses. Everybody had a mosquito bar, but that didn't keep out the bedbugs. We finally found out how to get rid of them. We would take a dozen egg whites in a bowl and add quicksilver.

Era said: You beat the egg whites up and put two or three tablespoons or so of quicksilver in the egg whites. With a chicken feather you paint the bed springs and all around the bedding. The bed bugs eat that heavy quicksilver and it stays in their little stomachs and it kills them.

Meese said: In spite of all the hardships we built that Tamiami Trail. I'm proud that I helped do it. It has to do with a big part of the history in southwest Florida. Those years we lived on that Trail at Royal Palm Hammock were good years. Lots of things happened out there.

Era remembered some special times. She said: The Indian children first played round us there. We sold the things the Indians made. This Indian, Bobby Clay and our son, Meece, Jr., played together all the time. They had their toy cars, wagons and bicycles. There was a road all the way around our building. They would take turns throwing a basketball into the hoop Meece put up. They would be riding their bicycles and make a basket, then ride on around. The next time the other one would make a basket.

Bobby didn't go to white man's school, so when he grew up he didn't want his children going to a white man's school. He didn't send his children.

Meece spoke up to say: Bobby was even taken to court and tried. Bobby won.

When we run the Royal Palm Hammock Station we had the only place for fishermen to stay. They stayed in our cottages to fish in Goodland and Marco. We had a lot of famous people who came. Ted Trueblood was one. He wrote for Field and Stream. Ray P. Holland lived in Naples. He was editor of Field and Stream. David Newell, too.

One of the people we had visit was Kermit Roosevelt. He and his wife and two little girls wanted to go down in the Everglades and the Ten Thousand Islands on a camping trip. They rented a boat in Goodland. They rented one of our cottages. He didn't know me from Adam's house cat, but he left their money, pocket book, jewelry, diamonds and everything there with me to put in our safe. Those days people could do that. Most people were honest. They really roughed it for two weeks.

Era proudly stated: We have two little granddaughters. Lessie and Jessie. Their parents are our son Meece, Jr. and his wife, Barbara Grant. His daddy had two wrecker businesses in town. We don't especially like Naples and Collier County now because we can't fit in with it anymore. It is too noisy for one thing. All our friends are dead.

We lived at Royal Palm Hammock, and across from our station lived two or three families of Indian parents and children. They were all related to Tom Buster. There was Charlie Billie and an Indian woman who was over 103 years old in 1923. There was an alligator that was 13 feet four inches that John and Harry Jumper caught. I bought that alligator and put it in the canal in front of the station for the tourists to see.

That house in Deep Lake Grove was the first in that country around there. It belonged to the banker Langford in Ft. Myers. Langford and his partner planted this 350-acre grove there, and in 1906 and 1907 we had a devastating freeze in the ridge section around Haines City. They wanted to get away from the cold – as far south as they could – for oranges and grapefruit.

Maria Stone ~ THE TAMIAMI TRAIL

I don't think there is anybody alive that knows this. The old, original road that came around from Marco Junction around by Royal Palm Hammock and down toward Carnestown was built in there to get that fruit out of there. They had a tram road from Everglades City out to Deep Lake. They were going to build that highway up to about where Carnestown is now, and load that fruit in trucks and bring it out. That was in 1915.

Now one of the boys that operated that dredge - was managin' a dragline - was Rosco Walker. He was brother to Forest Walker.

Let me tell you about the walking cousins. Lawton Chiles, Sr.'s mother was my father's sister. Lawton Chiles, Jr., is my second cousin. The paper said, . . . "then Senator Lawton Chiles, speaking at an old-timers gathering in Everglades City, had a visit with his cousin, Meece Ellis, pioneer of Collier County. Elected to the Senate in 1979, after walking the campaign over the whole state, Senator Chiles wore his fourth and last pair of walking shoes to the old-timer's gathering at Everglades semi-centennial." (Lawton Chiles is now Governor of Florida)

I was an employee of Collier Corporation in 1922 that operated the walking dredge that dug the canal to build the Tamiami Trail. He walked from town to town across the state; that's how he got elected. I walked the dredge across the state, too.

I became a Mason in 1927 at Everglades, the first Lodge in Collier County.

One time we had an 80-pound garfish. They figure it came around on the outside canal from Louisiana or Mississippi. I weighed fish in for the Metropolitan Fishing contest. We had a snook that weighed 20 pounds at the station at Royal Palm Hammock. We just had to go right outside our door to fish in those days - also to hunt.

Meece, Jr., our son, loved living at Royal Palm Hammock. After school in Naples, he'd take his rod and take off. He'd catch the small tarpon. We had all these fish pictures and mounted fish to show people who came to our cabins. We have some wonderful memories from Royal Palm Hammock. One was a picture of a big cypress bend on the trail in the full moon. Ed Trueblood took a picture of that spot.

I know a lot about this water business, myself, because I dug many canals on the Marion Floating Dredge, and every once in a while, we'd sink that dredge in 12 or 14 feet of water. We tried putting an earthen dam behind the dredge and using big pumps in there to pump the water out so we could float the dredge back. When we got the water pumped down to about three feet, the water would rush in there so fast. The rock is porous, and we just couldn't get the hole dry. That's the way all this country is all out to the Ramada Ranch and Golden Gate. That porous rock is underneath, and the water just goes right through.

Era said: We used to have nor'westers in the winter that brought a lot of rain. We don't have the rains we used to have.

Meece continued, the Colliers were very good to me. Miles Collier's daddy sold me property. I'm the first one that got to buy worthwhile property that they sold. I'm the first one in Collier County. They sold me that corner at Royal Palm Hammock. I worked for them from 1922 to 1937. I never worked for finer people.

Era said, I was the one who stayed on that dredge if Meece had to go elsewhere on his job. I had to be the big Marian Dredge-Keeper so he could keep his job. It was just wonderful. It was during the depression years. We got $130 a month. They furnished a truck and gasoline. We had eight rooms on the Marian Dredge. I was afraid. I was a little country girl and didn't want to live way out there, but what could I do? Meece taught me how to shoot a gun.

Meece said: She got too good with that 22 pistol and she was shooting alligators. There were lots of alligators near the Dredge. There were lots of snakes around the Dredge. She would shoot those snakes' heads off. She'd be on the porch up above and shoot down. When she shot an alligator, he sank, but in three or four days, he'd rise to the top all bloated up and it was up to me to get him out of the canal then.

Era said, We didn't need that smell around. Finally, he told me I couldn't shoot any more alligators. I got so I could beat him at target shooting so, soon we didn't want to target-shoot anymore. We were all girls in my family, and my daddy didn't have all those guns; we girls didn't care about that. It was a new life for me, and I learned a lot. We got married when I was 19, and we went to live on the Dredge pretty soon after we were married. We lived there five years like that. I told him if I hadn't been a country girl already and my daddy a farmer, I couldn't have toughed it out.

Meece's daddy lived at Fort Myers, and he was a great hunter; they would come almost ever weekend. I had to cook, cook, cook. I cooked venison and fish. The trout was muddy-tasting to me. Then they didn't filet that out.

Meece continued, We had a big garden on the land near the Dredge. We had chickens, ducks, geese, and guinea for awhile.

Era said, We didn't have a baby yet. We were married eight years before our son was born. Living on the Dredge was where I needed the baby. When Meece, Jr., was born, we were living in Everglades City. He was born in Fort Myers. That was before we got the station at Royal Palm Hammock. All those years there were good.

Meece said: I want to talk more about building the Tamiami Trail. When the Collier County got two Bay City dredges to head east from Carnestown, they soon ran into rock which had to be blasted by dynamite from there on. The dynamite was shipped from Tampa by boat.

All the staples came by boat from Tampa and some from Fort Myers, then they were transported by boat up the canal to the dredge camp. We only had ice, so some meat shipped to us was unfit to use.

In 1925, better refrigeration took care of our problem with fresh meat. Mr. Collier made sure we had the best cooks and plenty of food, so we never went hungry.

We had a big labor turnover because the work was so hard and the mosquitoes were terrible. Progress was slow the first two-and-a-half years. That was due to not using enough dynamiting, and breakdowns of dredge equipment. Graham Copeland took complete charge of the whole operation. He ordered the dynamite blasting to be increased and also better drilling methods to seat the dynamite. We made better progress from then on. We ran two ten-hour shifts each day, which moved us 75 to 100 feet in a 10-hour shift. This was a good distance for a small dredge in heavy rock.

We established two firsts. As I already told you, number one, we used four house trailers on this job. Each would sleep 12 men. The trailers were moved close to the dredges each time they moved. The mess hall was on barges in the canals. Number two "first" was the use of portable johns. They were big wooden nail kegs with the top and bottom knocked out. When you had to go to the bathroom, you took one off the dredge, put it down on the ground and sat down on it. You wouldn't waste anytime on the john. If you didn't use one, the mosquitoes and horse flies would tear your fanny up. Collier County owes a great debt to Barron Collier and his family.

"Doc" Johnson   W.J. Rutledge   Meece Ellis

THE DYNAMITE MAN
W. J. Rutledge

When first there was talk about putting the Tamiami Trail in, some people didn't want it and signed a petition to stop it. They didn't want the old Lee County split up into Collier County and Hendry County. Lee County wouldn't be so big if that was done. When we built the Trail we moved the dynamite by oxen. Oxen could walk in deep mud where horses or a tractor couldn't. When we got a roadbed, a tractor could run on it.

We used to call those boys from Georgia who came to work on the Trail "Pharo's Army." Some got paid and wanted to quit. Those oxen could pull that cart full of dynamite and gas right through that mud. The reason those men would want to quit was they got tired of standin' in the mud. They got paid once a month. They didn't work on Saturday and Sunday. On Saturday some would go to Turner's River where Bill House lived. He sold good whisky that he got from Nassau.

It was against the law to drink. Dan House, Bill's brother, would go to Nassau and bring it back. They sold it for five dollars a bottle. If anyone went there for whisky, Bill would say, "Give me five dollars, and I will tell you where I saw a bottle hid in the bushes on the little path that goes into the swamp." These two guys on Chokoloskee had me dynamite out that bay so they could get their liquor in there more easy. During a storm we had about sixty percent of the dynamite for the Trail was damaged, so it was sold to those old guys. They hired me to do the dynamite. When we were to build the Trail I was to dynamite the rocks. When you set off dynamite you don't look down. You look up. That way you can see where those rocks are going to fall. They fall to the outside, usually, so we move to the middle and look up.

When I was workin' on the Trail I ate venison until I was sick of it. Meece Ellis and John Doleson were crack shots. They would go up in the swamp toward Miami where there were lots of deer. We got one deer a week. I used to go to school with Meece's wife in Buckingham, Eura Mae Womble. We all knew each other back then.

I never told any woman I loved her but Alice. She is my wife. The food was so good I decided to take the cook. I married her.

One man that was killed on building the Trail happened this way. He was up on the boom to the dragline. The boy named Earl Ivey he had on there thought the man told him to move the boom. The man fell down off that dragline and busted his head wide open. He had a wife and children. Earl Ivey's wife run the Ivey boarding house in Everglades.

Barron Collier came to the Tram Road once. I saw him out there. He and all his sons were fine men. He asked me to take care of his house and yard. It wasn't enough money, so I went to work in Buckingham building a camp for those soldier boys.

Of the eighty-two years of my life, the most important thing I've done is to raise two girls and a son. That boy was only two and a half years old when I married my wife. His name is David Weeks, and I love him, and he loves me.

Barron Collier built the Trail. I just worked on it because he paid me. The old Trail was like a washboard. If you drove fifty miles an hour on the old Trail you'd shake to death, but it was a good road.

There was a junction to go to Marco then turned and went to Palm Hammock. The road went through Belle Meade. When we first come here we had to go by a junction. One went on to Marco. You got on the boat at Caxambas, and then took the mail truck into Naples. You could ride back, get on that boat and they would take you to Everglades City where the Post Office was. Even then when you come to the junction you would come around to Palm Hammock and down to Carnestown and on in to Everglades.

There was this Tram Road to Deep Lake. Barron Collier built it the way it is now. Cuttin' the cypress trees and sellin' land helped pay for the Trail, I think. I worked on Collier Company twenty-five years doin' lumber countin', dirt rocks and muck. I cut grass for seventeen years after I retired.

I WAS ON FIRE
Dinks Bogges

I was born January 16, 1910 in Everglades City.

When the boat blew up with me it broke nine windows three blocks away from that boat in a hotel and some houses. That was at a little dock in Ft. Myers, Florida. There were three on that boat. I'm the only one livin,' Dode Russell and one more fellow.

It was a homemade gas tank. It had ten thousand gallons of gas aboard. I was hauling it to Everglades City for the Collier Corporation. We started to pull out, and the boat blew up. Dode was blowed up in the air and fell across the railroad tracks and he was broke all up. He didn't get burned.

I was on fire. I was burned bad. It burned my ears off. I came up in the water. The gasoline was on fire on the water. I come through the fire. Benny Alderman picked me up. He was workin' on a new boat at the dock. When there was the explosion they told him he couldn't go out in his new boat because it hadn't been checked out yet. Benny said, "There is somebody out there hollerin' in the fire and I've gotta go."

Benny went out in his new boat through the fire. He reached down and grabbed me (Dinks) in the water and brought me up from that fire all around. The skin was slipping from my arms. I said, "You ain't hurtin' me," so he went ahead and picked me up. I was numb. I was blind for six weeks.

Mr. Collier had an ice basket sent from Tampa. When the ambulance came they could only carry one person. Dode said, "You take Dinks because he is hurt worse than I am." I couldn't see, but I walked off the dock by bein' led to the ambulance.

I've lived in Everglades City all my life. I lived across from Sunset Lodge. There was the schoolhouse and two houses and a little piece of high land. Them days there wasn't no fill there.

Dinks daughter spoke up to say: After that, my daddy built a six-room house on Sand Fly Pass. They call it Bogges Island now. His daddy grew tomatoes on San Fly Pass. That's where the tour boats go today. My father is the third of seven children.

Dinks said: My parents were Charles and Ethel Bogges. Hilda is married to Gandees. Then there was Alvin, then me, Frieda, Loraine, Elveta and Clifton. They are all dead but me.

Dinks continued: We put those tomatoes we grew on the New York market in three days from Sand Fly Pass. We floated them ourselves to Key West and put them on a big steamboat named *Tide Line*. They went straight to New York from Key West non-stop. We got a big price for our tomatoes. When he wasn't farmin' Dad went to Boca Grande to be a charter boat guide for tarpon fishin.' I run a boat for haulin' groceries over to Collier's Hotel on Useppa Island.

We had two inches more floodwater than the storm of 1910 had. One person drowned in that storm. I was in a little open boat with a little spray hood on it. There were eight or nine of us. I miss being on the water.

In 1929 I was in a storm. I run a tugboat for Mr. Barron Collier. He was a good man. He took care of his people. I used to go to Caxambas to pick him up and carry him to Everglades City.

THE TAMPA KID & OUR MEMORIES OF THE TRAIL
Alto Griffin and Hazel Griffin

When the Tamiami Trail was being built my job was to run the grader behind a tractor to smooth out the roadway. I also drove a truck that hauled shell and cordwood. After the Trail was built I had trucks that hauled shell for the upkeep of the Trail. I had a garage at Ochopee. There I had a wrecker that pulled people out of the canals and wrecks along the Trail.

My wife, Hazel, had the Poinciana Grill in Ochopee. She had cabins to rent, too. Hazel and I were lucky to be a part of the building and life along this historic Tamiami Trail. Building the Trail amid the alligators, snakes, mosquitoes, muck and noise and boredom was altered by one event: that of the Tampa Kid's escape.

The state prison department maintained a convict camp halfway between Carnestown and what was later Royal Palm Hammock near CR #92 and US #41 today. The purpose of this camp was to provide manual labor for the building of bridges along the Tamiami Trail. From time to time the convicts numbered fifty to more than seventy. These men were unmistakable as they worked along the Trail because they wore the traditional black and white stripped uniforms.

These were black prisoners serving life sentences for terrible crimes. They wore leg irons and armed guards stood nearby at all times to prevent shirking work or escaping. One or so did escape into the wild Everglades but were glad to return, for life out there was worse than camp life.

Captain Hansford was hired by the State DOT to control and work the prisoners. The prisoner known as Tampa Kid had one goal in mind and that was to escape. He had attempted escapes at least twice.

Figuring he had a ghost of a chance he, as leader, and his cronies made their getaway one early afternoon during the hot summer of 1927. Tampa Kid had been watching for his chance. The guard over him fell asleep and dropped his shotgun on his knees. The Kid saw his chance and grabbed the guard's shotgun and side arm.

The sleeping guard woke up to find himself a hostage. Tampa Kid and his four buddies then forced the three other guards to give up their weapons. Tampa Kid pulled down nearby phone lines. By that time a "trusty" came along in a truck. They forced him to drive his truck toward Royal Palm Hammock. Just before getting to Royal Palm Hammock a car driven by Mr. Williams, manager of Inter-County Telephone Company, came along. The Tampa Kid had his hostage "trusty" driver block the road with the truck.

The gang got into Mr. Williams' car and continued on. At Royal Palm Hammock they took the old shell road that went through Marco to Naples. They went a short way and met the engineer from Punta Gorda from Florida State Road Department. He didn't know what was happening so he pulled off the one-lane road and waved them by and on they went. He wasn't suspicious because convicts were used by all the crews working on the Trail.

Tampa Kid and his buddies went through Naples, then Estero and on to Ft. Myers. Bill Clark, later the Mayor of Naples, had a crew cutting pilings. His car with the keys in it was parked nearby. The convicts forced Mr. Williams into Bill's car and they took off leaving the other car with a part missing. Bill's car threw a bearing, so they blocked the one-way rut with it and waited for another car to come along. This time it was a salesman who they made dump his goods, and they continued on through Ft. Myers in his car.

When they came to the old Slater Sawmill the Kid got out and forced the blacksmith to cut his leg irons off. He released his hostages here, too. This was his downfall as they soon spread the word. Along came a motor-powered handcar carrying a railroad crew. The convicts drew their guns and took the railroad handcar. This was up by Fort Ogden. They ran out of gas in a short distance. The convicts had to "hole up" in the nearby swamp. By then word spread about what had happened and a posse was organized. They were found hiding in the swamp and a shootout took place. Three convicts were killed. Tampa Kid fell in the gun battle, too. The other two convicts gave up with their leader gone. Well, one convict was the "trusty" who drove the truck so he was really forced to go along for the ride. Tampa Kid got his wish after all.

Now I remember once at the camp Tampa Kid told me that he was a crackerjack wood carver. He kept wanting my knife to whittle something for me. I had my gun on him and I let him carve with my knife. He did a beautiful pipe with a big bowl. He told me that he carved a .38 out of wood and blacked it with shoe polish. It looked so real that he robbed a bank in Tampa with it. He liked to talk about the bad things he had done. He always said he would die escaping.

One thing for sure, he created some excitement for us working on the Trail. He got away with passing all those people because it wasn't unusual to see someone with a load of convicts going somewhere. Well, that was Tampa Kid.

Alto began: I had the garage in Ochopee. Lots of people came along the Trail, even famous people. I knew the guy with the bushy eyebrows, John L. Lewis, who was in Miami. I had seen it in the paper. Well, one day this big Cadillac drove up and had a chauffeur. I gassed him up and John L. Lewis got out of the car. I especially noticed how his eyebrows run together. I asked if he got good mileage, etc. I just kept talking, and I never could get that man to say a word to me. The only thing he did say was, "Give me a receipt for that." I've always been able to get a conversation out of everybody I ever talked to, but I couldn't get no conversation out of him.

During the time Al Capone was in Prison, Al Capone's son, about ten years old, come by the garage in Ochopee. He didn't know his daddy was in prison. He thought he was just off somewhere. He had a bodyguard with him. This bodyguard had brought him out along the Trial to shoot this rifle he had. The plunger come out of this little rifle, and he lost it. The guard said, "I've talked to some of the boys, and they think you might be able to fix it for him." He was a pretty good-sized man. I thought that the boy was his at first. I took it back in the garage and fixed it for the kid. He was pretty happy about that. He shot it a couple of times. I charged him about a dollar.

When the boy went on out to the car the man said, "That is Al Capone's son, and I'm his bodyguard. He don't get to shoot a gun in Miami, so I brought him out to shoot. He don't know his daddy is in prison. He thinks he is off somewhere. We don't tell him."

Hazel said: Al Capone had a big club out in Pine Crest, down the Trail from Ochopee at Loop Road.

Alto said: I never was at it; I just passed down through there.

Hazel said: There was a lot of fun going on out there.

Alto said: If they came among us we didn't know who they were.

Hazel said: This little old lady came by out restaurant kinda late one night. She had been hired by somebody to go down on Loop Road to work on the Chicken Ranch. She was hitchhiking. We talked her into not going, and to stay there with us. We ended up hiring her. Her name was Vera.

Alto said: I named her Button and Bows. She was a dry little old thing, but she was wonderful to talk to. She used to work for some movie stars in Hollywood. She went with them to Las Vegas. While they gambled she held their furs and bags. She loved to tell jokes.

We had cottages, and she took care of the linens. She also went up to Immokalee to take care of our things there later on.

This happened at our place in Ochopee. There was a woman that killed her baby. She had just broke up with her husband and rented a cottage from us, and she killed it there. I was working at Lee Memorial Hospital at night, and got off at 7:00 A.M. I would drive home in the early morning. This woman had cut her wrist, and Alto and the Deputy Sheriff, Kent Feathers, was taking her to Ft. Myers Hospital. They stopped me on the road and told me not to go over to that cottage, that the woman they had in the car had killed her baby in that cottage. When I got home Vera said, "I was hoping they wouldn't tell you. You need to get to bed and get some rest."

Well, who is going to rest when you find out there is a little dead baby lying in the house behind the one you are in. I was working in the hospital, so I saw plenty. Vera was going to protect me.

Just then somebody knocked on the door. It was the Deputy Sheriff, Doug Hendry. He wouldn't go in the cottage. He asked me if I would go in there and pick out some clothes for it as the ambulance was going to take it somewhere.

He said, "I can't look at it. I can't stand it."

The woman took the pillowcase and twisted it and wrapped it around the baby's neck. Its head was black and swollen. It was terrible. The baby was a year or so old. She told that she asked him if he wanted to go to heaven and he said, "Yes." She came in from somewhere. She rented for just one night. I guess that was why she wanted the cottage. It was a terrible experience for all concerned.

Hazel remembers the convict camp: The convict camp was located where Weaver's Way Station was built when the Trail was opened. That is where the convict camp was. The Tampa Kid was kept with about 70 other convicts. One was called Sandy Bottom. Besides running the road grader behind a tractor, Alto would drive the truck and take the prisoners into camp. They had to be in before dark.

One time one other truck turned over and went in the canal. It had a load of rocks and dirt. The driver and one prisoner I know of got buried. Alto got out of his truck and stood back with his gun loaded and pointed at the prisoners. Alto made Sandy Bottom get the other prisoners in the canal and dig those people out of the dirt and rock. Sandy Bottom was a big black prisoner. The other prisoners were afraid of him. He could boss them around. He was a bad man and the others were afraid of him.

Alto got to come home on Saturdays from working on the Trail. Some Sunday mornings we would get up and go down to the camp. We would take the baby with us. There was a boxing ring fixed up for the prisoners. The prisoners would do boxing and people would come out from Everglades and around to see them. It wasn't a good road, but they had it fixed up enough so people could come out from Everglades to the prison camp.

There was one prisoner who took care of the baby for me quite a bit. His name was Tony. I trusted him to take care of my baby. He wasn't going to hurt my baby. Besides, there was all those people around there with guns on them. Those prisoners weren't going to do anything.

Tony was a cook. The prisoners ate in a place that had a partition between them and where we ate. The partition had wide cracks and we could see the prisoners. Tony cooked good venison. He would fix it special for me. Sunday visitors ate at the table where the guards ate. Tony would hold my baby while I ate my dinner. That was the first time a black person had ever held my baby. They wore stripes and had on chains.

You know, Tampa Kid broke loose. He said he'd never come back to camp. He said they could kill him because he wasn't going to live there anymore. Mosquitoes were bad down there.

There was a community house at Everglades across from the Everglades Inn when they dug the canals. I don't remember the occasion, but we were there. A banister separated the section where the black people sat from where the white people sat. I'll never forget that night because I enjoyed their music so much. Those prisoners sat over there and they were singing songs. One was When The Saints Come Marchin' In. That was the first time I ever remember hearing that song. They sang the different parts in harmony. It was just beautiful.

The guards there worried that night about getting them back to camp because it was so dark. I don't remember what it was but something special went on that day, but I can't remember what it was.

There was a sweatbox there at camp if any of them needed punishing. It was a big box that they were put in and the lid was fastened down. They had to stay in that place without much air. There was some guy called Captain Hansford who was in charge of all these prisoners.

If my husband ever had any trouble with the prisoners I don't believe he would have told me. We weren't talking prisoners when we got together. This was about 1927. People had been working on the Trail from Dade County, too when Alto and I were dating thirteen months before we got married in September of 1925. We went down where the Trail was being built. The first time I went down on the Trail the grade was thrown up this side of Carnestown. We couldn't get in to Everglades but we could get to Carnestown. The sand was all piled up on the other side toward Ochopee and you couldn't get to Everglades.

When Alto and I were dating we went down there and crossed Turner's River Bridge. They just had the framework there and just had the two by sixes for you to drive across. You had to be sure your wheels stayed on the boards or you went in the river. There were some Indians sitting at the end. They had something cooked for their supper. We got out and took pictures of them.

We Old Timers remember all about the building of the Tamiami Trail.

Griffin operated a gas station in Ochopee, a few miles east of Carnestown on the way to Miami along the Trail. In the 1930s this was a thriving tomato farming community and their Poinsettia Grill was a popular restaurant.

TAMIAMI TRAIL HISTORY

Colonel Frank F. Tenney, Jr. (USAF Ret.)
An in-depth look at a remarkable engineering achievement accomplished
here in Collier County between 1926 & 1928.

This article first appeared in the Collier County Heritage Magazine, *a publication of the Collier County Historical Society. It is used in its entirety with the permission of its writer.*

Although the Tamiami Trail was first conceived way back in the 1910's, hardly a mile of first class highway existed in Collier County when the County was carved out of Lee County in 1923. This was due to the fact that the State of Florida then had a very impractical policy on road building. Each community was expected to establish a road and bridge district and sell bonds to finance road construction within its boundaries. This worked fine in populous counties like Dade where they were able to complete their 43 miles or 15.6% of the 273 miles Trail by 1918. In Collier County with a population of only 1265, in the 1925 census, it was quite another matter.

Based largely on Mr. Barron Collier's promise to get the Tamiami Trail construction going again, the 1923 Legislature acted favorably on his request to create Collier County. He lost no time getting work underway, but he faced a formidable task. Seventy-six miles or 28% of the Trail fell in Collier County. From a point several miles west of Carnestown to the Dade County Line there was nothing but untamed Everglades. By October 1923 he had a one cubic yard Marion floating dredge working east from Carnestown and on January 1924 he started a one cubic yard Bay City crawler east from Carnestown.

At that period the Florida land boom was at its peak and workmen were hard to keep on a job. At times labor turnover ran as high as 50% per month. One time when someone asked Mr. Collier how many shifts he used, he only half jokingly replied "Three – One coming down from Tampa, one on the job, and one on the way back to Tampa." All this would end in 1926 when the Florida recession started and dependable workers would be happy just to have a job.

With all the adversity it is not surprising that by the fall of 1926, after having spent more than one million dollars, Mr. Collier still had 31 miles of Trail to be constructed from the dredge on the east Trail to the Dade County Line. To make matters worse he would soon find that 31 miles would have to be cut through solid rock, not the nice easy sand they had encountered up to this point.

There was one faint ray of hope on the horizon. Back in the 1925 Governor's race, John W. Martin had made a pledge to complete the Tamiami Trail within his administration and he won the election. Unlike so many politicians today, he intended to keep that pledge. In August 1926 the State of Florida took over the Tamiami Trail project in Collier County and the word went out "come hell or high water complete the Tamiami Trail".

Very soon thereafter the nine men, who would organize the first State Road Department Engineering Crew, started to arrive in Everglades. W.R. "Bob" Wilson, who lived in Naples arrived there on Sept. 16, 1926, two days before the great hurricane of 1926.

We are indebted to him for much of the information that appears in this story. Mr. Thomas L. "Tommy" Stephens also arrived about that time to become project engineer. Previously he had been an engineer in Nicaragua with the United Fruit Company. Since he was an avid photographer he took many of the photographs you will see in this book.

The mission of the State Road Department Engineering Crew was to run the grade lines for the Trail and supervise the carrying out of the terms of the contract.

By the time the State took over control, the construction firm of Alexander, Ramsey and Kerr, with D. Graham Copeland as chief engineer, were ready to move into high gear. They had dredged the shallow winding Barron River into a wide deep waterway capable of handling ocean-going vessels. A canal had been built up to Carnestown to connect with the canal on the east Trail so that gasoline and other bulk supplies could be moved to the "front" down these canals on narrow barges. Back at the Everglades, a port facility and shops had been built upstream from the city at a place called Port DuPont. It had a large machine shop, foundry, repair garage, electric shop, woodworking plant and a shipyard. These facilities could repair or rebuild any machinery used on the Trail. Twenty highly skilled workers ran this facility under Mr. H.L. Briston, a very experienced mechanical engineer. In addition there were living quarters and messing facilities for workers. Had these facilities not been available the State would most certainly have had to have constructed such a facility before work on the Trail could have been accelerated.

D. Graham Copeland, a 1906 graduate of the United States Naval Academy at Annapolis resigned from the service after WWII and was selected by Mr. Collier to become his chief engineer. Having had long military experience, naturally he set up his organization along military lines. A nerve center was established back at Everglades with phone lines to the "front". As they advanced, the phone lines were extended so that progress could be constantly monitored. The moment any equipment failed, repair crews sprang into action to work around the clock to make repairs. Because there was very little storage space at the front, supplies had to be sent to the front daily in just the right amounts. The project can best be compared to a scaled down "Panama Canal" project. It ran round the clock with every man expected to put forth his best effort at all times.

What makes the whole project all the more remarkable was that the construction firm of Alexander, Ramsay and Kerr at the same time had an even larger, but less well publicized, project underway. They were simultaneously building a road and a railroad bed down from Immokalee to Everglades. Since Everglades was completely isolated from Immokalee by 40 miles of tropical Everglades, it was necessary to establish a duplicate of the facilities at Port DuPont at the rail head in Immokalee. Mr. C.G. Wilson was the engineer in charge of the Immokalee Division and was pretty much on his own with only telephone communications to the "Nerve Center: at Everglades.

Basically both operations at the front were the same except that on the Immokalee road a 40' wide 15' deep canal had to be dug in order to provide enough fill to build both a road and a railroad bed. On the east Trail a 20' wide, 15' deep canal provided enough fill for that project. We will first explain how the Tamiami Trail was built, then at the end of the article we will point out where the Immokalee Road project differed.

The first operation on both "fronts" was to lay out the center line of the road. Rod men had to blaze the Trail by cutting down the brush with machetes, then stakes were driven in the ground every 100' to mark the center of the road.

They had to traverse almost impossible terrain to accomplish this, fording streams and crossing wide rivers. On the east Trail this was done sometime before 1923 because the "Trail Blazers" who crossed the Everglades that year in Model "T" Fords tried to follow the line the surveyors had run.

Bob Wilson tells an amusing tale about one of his first days on the job back in 1926. He walked from the end of the grade in Collier County clear to the Dade County Line – alone. His biggest problem was finding the stakes that marked the center line. The Survey Team had used lathes for markers which over the years had rotten off near the ground. He had to find the short stub sticking out of the ground surrounded by deep sawgrass. Then he had to re-mark the location with new states cut from brush, an almost endless job. After he finished that long walk he found out that a character named "Bum Bum" Monroe was supposed to have accompanied him, but sent him out alone to "test out their new man".

Next came the clearing crew. All trees had to be cut down, using 2-man hand saws, and dragged clear of the right of way by teams of oxen. Some giant cypress trees were as much as 7' in diameter. Many times this work had to be done by men standing in waist deep water and muck. Large trees were later salvaged and taken to a sawmill to be cut into timber for use in building bridges. Scrub brush which, abounded in the area, had to be cut by hand using machetes. An occasional encounter with rattlesnakes up to 7 ½' in length added zest to the job. The clearing crew had their own camp way out ahead of the dredge and supplies were brought in by ox team. The cost of clearing the right of way ran from $75 to $300 an acre.

Once clearing had been accomplished, standard gauge industrial rails were laid for a marvelous drilling machine which had been designed specifically for this job and built in the shop back at Port DuPoint. Mounted on a special railway car were two Ingersoll-Rand Compressors used to drive the three pneumatic drills mounted six feet apart across the front of the machine. Each drill was sixteen feet long and since they had to be perfectly vertical in order to keep the drill from binding, it was necessary to jack up the rail on the low side to level the car before drilling could start. Three holes were drilled simultaneously about twelve feet into solid rock then the drills were lifted out of the ground, the holes were marked with sticks and the car advanced six feet to drill three more holes. Bob Wilson said that the three drills and the two compressors all running at the same time made so much noise it made your ears ache.

Since only one of these machines were available on the East Trail it was run continuously day and night for 28 months averaging about two-hundred-fifty feet of forward progress each day. The Ingersoll-Rand Co. was good enough to furnish R.H. Cunningham, manager of their Birmingham, Ala. Office and Mr. A.H. Sellars of the rock drilling department in New York to make recommendations on the most efficient employment of the drilling equipment. As the drilling machine advanced, the rails were to support advanced, the rails used to support this 30-ton machine were taken up and relaid ahead of the machine. Since the rate of advance of this machine set the pace for all the rest of the operation, it was vital to keep this machine advancing.

By the time the blasting crew arrived, almost always the holes had become filled with water and muck. It was therefore necessary to flush them out with jetting pumps. For this purpose two Fairbanks Morse units were used. The discharge from these pumps was reduced to a 5/8 inch double strength pipe fourteen feet long. Once the holes were cleaned out from 10 to 40 sticks of 60% nitroglycerine dynamite was dropped into each hole. The harder the rock the more sticks of dynamite it was necessary to use. For 2 miles west of the Dade County Line it was necessary to use 40 sticks in each center hole and 20 sticks in the side holes. Once five or six hundred pounds of dynamite was set the blasting crew retreated from the area and fired the charge thus breaking the solid rock into small enough chunks for the dredge to throw out of the canal.

Getting the dynamite to the front was a major logistical problem. It was shipped from the factory to the railhead at Ft. Myers by freight car. One entire freight car load was used every 3 weeks for three years. From Fort Myers to Everglades it was transported by barge. From Everglades to the front it was moved by barge then stored in a magazine well away from the living area. It was moved from the magazine to the blasting area by ox team whenever possible. This was also true of the gasoline needed to keep the drilling machines and jetting pumps in operation. At all times an average of 40 oxen were available. The average time an ox was used under these extremely adverse conditions was 2 weeks. During 1927, 29 oxen were either killed or injured. At some places the muck became so deep oxen couldn't traverse it. It was then necessary to lay wooden rails and men pushed a car loaded with dynamite to the blasting area. A very slow laborious process indeed. At one point it was even necessary to resort to loading supplies on a flat bottom boat and pushing it through the water and muck.

To construct the 31-mile stretch of the trail from Carnestown to the Dade County Line required more than 2,584,000 sticks of dynamite. If these sticks had been placed end to end they would have stretched all the way from Tampa, Florida to San Francisco, California. The cost of dynamite alone represented 50% of the total cost of construction on that section of the Trail. The cost could have been much higher without the full cooperation of the Hercules Powder Company. They sent an engineer on an inspection trip to the front every two months to keep in touch with the blasting progress and recommend ways to improve blasting efficiency. It is a tribute to the safety standards employed that not a man lost his life handling and firing this huge amount of high explosive. Only one man was injured by a blast, but the long time it took him to reach a hospital demonstrated how serious a bad accident in this remote area could have been. He was first transported by car to Everglades to receive first aid at the clinic. After than he had to be transported by special boat to Ft. Myers to enter the hospital where he received further treatment.

Once the rock had been broken up by blasting, the Bay City Dredge arrived on the scene. These huge machines had treads wide apart so they could straddle the relatively narrow twenty foot canal and throw up the rock as they moved ahead. Three of thee dredges were used in tandem to speed up the work. They employed a system of leap froging. The first machine would advance 400' and start work, the second machine would advance about 200' and go to work, while the rear machine would start work where the canal ended. Once they ran out of rock to dredge the whole process was repeated and all machines advanced about 400'. The canal was dug about twenty feet wide and as deep as the bucket would reach, which was about fifteen feet. Every once in a while a dredge would run across a boulder much too big to be lifted. This was caused by one of the holes failing to fire. It then became necessary to re-shoot in front of the dredge. Two bundles of dynamite with 40 sticks each were tired by an electric blasting cap placed between them. This reduced the boulder to many small pieces which the dredge could handle.

Any rocks that the dredge could lift that were above specifications had to be discarded on the north side of the canal. Many of these huge boulders may still be seen from the road as you drive on the East Trail.

Working in solid rock, as hard as granite, was extremely hard on these dredges. The one cubic yard buckets had an average useful life of only 2 weeks. A supply of teeth for the buckets were always kept on hand at the front so they could be replaced as they became broken.

The dredges worked two 10-hour shifts per day. Two hours were scheduled between shifts to carry out a rigid service, inspection, and maintenance program which drastically reduced breakdowns. Its purpose was to spot worn parts well in advance of the time they would break down. New parts could then be ordered from the factory and replaced before a breakdown occurred. The cables were forever breaking, causing the boom to drop straight down. Several hours were needed to replace it. When breakdowns did occur the repair crews worked round the clock to get the equipment back in working condition. Because every machine at the front was like a link in a chain, once a machine stopped every thing behind it had to stop. For the most part, repair crews were able to make repairs right on the spot. If a new part, not in stock, was needed the machine shops back at Port DuPont sprung into action to fabricate the new part in the foundry. The part was then finished in the machine shop. This procedure saved weeks of time waiting for a new part to be delivered from the factory.

Each Bay City dredge averaged 80 feet per shift. The three dredges averaged almost 1-½ miles of completed canal per month. The completed canal served two very useful functions. It provided drainage to keep the completed road from flooding after a heavy rain and it provided rock fill for the roadbed. Dredging had to be done very accurately. Each linear foot of canal would produce an average of five cubic yards of fill. In order to meet strict state road department specifications on the depth of road bed, exactly the correct amount of fill had to be thrown up for each foot of road bed.

The machines at the front used 10,000 gallons of gasoline and 2,000 gallons of fuel oil each week. This huge amount of fuel was transported by tanker from the Standard Oil Co. plant at Ft. Myers to Everglades, then by barge through the canal to the front where it was used.

In some sandy sections additional rock had to be brought in, frequently over quite some distance, to correct the deficiency of rock fill. It then became necessary to establish a rock quarry where rock was available. Then rails had to be laid and the fill was loaded on cars for transportation to the front. Mr. H.L. Bristol, who was in charge of all of the shops at Port DuPont, had designed and built the little locomotive used in this operation. Previously they had tried to use an old logging locomotive which proved to be too heavy for the rails causing them to buckle. Mr. Bristol locomotive was built around a four-cylinder Stearns motor from an old tractor. It proved to be ideal for the purpose. Once the required amount of fill had been thrown up by the dredge or brought in from a quarry, the pile of fill was ready to be shaped into a road bed.

A marvelous machine called the Bay City Skimmer Scoop levelled the pile of fill thus doing the work of at least 50 men. Today we would use a bulldozer to accomplish the same job. Only one of these machines was available on the East Trail so it too was used night and day to keep up with the dredges and was considered one of the most critical pieces of equipment at the front. By the time this machine had passed, a wide nearly level roadbed had been formed over which wheeled vehicles could pass.

At this point the grading crews took over. They were in charge of the mobile camp which they were required to keep within 2000' of the skimmer scoop. This meant that the camp would move ahead just about every 7 days.

Bob Wilson recalls that Mr. Lewis Thorpe (who later served Collier County as sheriff from 1928 until his untimely death in 1953) was grading superintendent on the east front. His good wife, who still lives in Naples, took a very active interest in how the food was prepared and how clean the living quarters were kept. Bob says it cost $1.25 a day for the surveyors to stay at any of the camps when they were in the field. The food they served was just the sort of food he had as a boy growing up on a farm. Good solid food that would stick to your ribs.

The camp on wheels provided 3 mess sections as portable bunkhouses for all men working at the front. Clean fresh food and ice was brought to the front daily from the commissary back at Port DuPont. To supplement this diet venison and wild turkey were purchased from the Indians who lived and hunted in the area. Permanently assigned mess attendants, usually women, prepared and served highly nutritious fresh prepared meals for this round the clock operation. This kept the morale high at the front.

Every effort was made to encourage the men to push on at top speed. The following sign was posted by the roadside not far east of Carnestown: *(see photo on page 33)*

TAMIAMI TRAIL HISTORY
THE FAMOUS 'ROCKY' ROAD TO DUBLIN
HAS SOME SOFT SPOTS BUT EVERY INCH
OF THIS SECTION OF THE TAMIAMI
TRAIL IS BLASTED FROM SOLID ROCK.
NOT CONTENT WITH SMASHING ROCK,
FRED DIDDEN AND HIS OUTFIT AT THIS
POINT OCTOBER 1, 1925 BEGAN
SMASHING ROCK-DREDGING RECORDS.
AVERAGE PROGRESS TO DATE IS
80 FEET PER DREDGE PER DAY. WATCH
EACH SHIFT CARVE OUT 100 FEET PER DAY.
ON TO MIAMI
THE TAMIAMI TRAIL BUILDER

With the road bed down it now became necessary to improve the surface so that it would meet strict Florida State Road Department specifications. They stipulated that no rocks larger than two inches in diameter could be within six inches of the surface and no rocks larger than six inches in diameter could be within one foot of the surface. The largest and heaviest scarifier made by Austin Western Co. With a fourteen-foot blade along which six-inch square steel teeth were spaced, either broke up or brought the larger rocks to the surface so they could be discarded. Bob Wilson remembered the first day they tried to use a smaller eight-foot scarifier pulled by a 5-ton tractor. Mr. G.C. Washbrun, who was Mr. Copeland's assistant, said, "I am sure that little machine will work just fine." Well they started the machine up and within 10 feet every tooth was pointing straight back. That ended any effort to use small machines on that tough rock.

Early in the game Mr. Copeland called Bob Wilson into his office and asked him to work with Mr. Thorpe to learn the details of the grading operation in case if became necessary to set up more grading teams. This was necessary he said because he didn't have any one in the company with enough construction experience. As a result, Bob learned how to grade from a real expert that he found very useful later in his career.

Next came the Austin Western rough graded with a fourteen foot steel blade pulled by a 10-ton tractor. Gradually the roadbed was upgraded until the surface was smooth. Fine grading consisted of re-working the surface until it was as smooth as a table top, at which point an asphalt surface was applied to prevent erosion.

The cost of building the trail increased steadily as they approached the Dade County Line because the rock became harder and more dynamite had to be used. The negotiated contract for the last section worked out to $2.12 per cubic yard for the completed road. This was fantastically high when the going rate for sand fill at that time was only $.25 per yard. Labor was very cheap in those days. Common laborers received $.20 per hour. Bob Wilson remembers his salary was $250.00 a month and his supervisor received $200.00 per month, both considered very high pay for the time.

The total cost of completing 31 miles of the East Trail was almost 8 million dollars. Or just about $25,000.00 per mile. A huge sum in those days, but only a fraction of what it would cost today.

One interesting operation that was started just about the time the Trail was finished was setting up the Southwest Mounted Police. Stations were established just about 10 miles apart at Belle Meade, Royal Palm Hammock, Weaver's Camp, Turner River, Monroe Station and Paolita just beyond 40-mile bend. Each station was manned by a husband and wife team. The husband was given a motorcycle and the wife was responsible for maintaining the station and selling soft drinks and gasoline. The mission of the police was not to catch bootleggers or robbers, but to assist motorists who had their motor car break down on the road, which happened very frequently in those days. Bob Wilson remembers the operation had a very tragic first year. Four of the policemen were killed in motorcycle accidents. One hit a bridge abutment, the next one hit a chuckhole and was thrown to his death. A third passed a car in a fog and hit a car head on. The last got his head knocked off on the road north of Naples. Bob blames inexperience for all of the accidents.

Operation of the Immokalee Division was similar to the East Trail except they had access to a railhead at Immokalee. (On the East Trail the nearest railhead was Ft. Myers 80 miles away.) Because they were building two roadbeds at the same time it made it necessary to provide twice as much fill so the canal was dug 40 feet wide. This made it practical to use a gigantic 3 ½ cubic yard Marion floating dredge with a 100-foot boom. Huge outriggers were necessary to keep the machine upright when the 110-foot boom was extended to its limit. As luck would have it, the summer following the 1926 Hurricane brought on an extreme drought dropping the water in the canal so much it became necessary to dam the canal and pump underground water into it to refloat the dredge. Huge brush fires were a constant threat that summer.

Instead of using a camp on wheels as was done on the East Trail, their camp was on a barge tied up to the bank near the dredge. The pictures that follow show some interesting aspects of this construction job where the road and railroad ran side by side for 40 miles.

1923 to 1928: From wilderness to a road through the glades.

The Echols and Ayres family operated the laundry which washed linens for the Rod & Gun Club and the Everglades Inn as well as cleaning uniforms of the staff who kept Collier's little town so immaculate. After World War II, the laundry ceased to operate and the building was used as offices. Eventually the Women's Club bought it and, realizing they could not maintain it, raised funds to create the Museum of the Everglades which opened on April 26, 1998, as the first satellite in the Collier County Museum system.

LIVING IN THE LAUNDRY
Lurleen Echols Chesser

I was born in Roanoke, Alabama. I came to Everglades City in 1933. Our mother had died in 1931.

There wasn't much work in Alabama. Well, Everglades couldn't pay too much either. They had the laundry and dry cleaning place that has now been turned into the Everglades Museum. My sister Ann and I came to Everglades in the back of this little laundry truck. It had no windows in it, and I couldn't see where we were going. My uncle, Ralph Echols, came up there and asked me did I want a job. He was helping Aunt Lois Ayers run the laundry and dry cleaning which, of course, Barron Collier had charge of, and everything else.

Well, I thought I was coming to the end of the world. When I got there I about decided I had. Anyway, all we had to do on a Sunday afternoon in Everglades was walk around and go for a boat ride. I lived in that laundry place after I came down. I slept there on a cot. Daytime we pushed it up under the table. I worked there for $3 a week, cash and board. The rest of my sisters came on down eventually. I led the way.

Harley Chesser called up and wanted to know if I wanted to come out to a dance. Aunt Lois said, "If they need to come to a dance I'll take them," meaning me and Ann. Well, my aunt took us to the dance. Mildred Mooney was running the telephone in Everglades. She called up one time and said, "I need somebody to go on a blind date tonight. I need you and Ruby." By that time sister Ruby had come down. I went on the blind date, but I didn't ever expect I'd see that man again. We had to double date with Bill Daughtry. He had the car Harley had just sold him the week before that date. It was a Model-A Ford.

On that date was Mildred Mooney, Ruby my sister, and me. The boys were Ward Morrison, Bill Daughtry and Harley Chesser. The irony of the thing, we came to Naples that first night. I jumped out of the car and tore my skirt. That didn't set too well with my aunt. "What kind of a guy was this you went out with, that you come home with your skirt all tore up?"

I said, "Oh, that's no problem. Anyway, Harley asked me if I was married. I said 'Yeah, I'm married.'"

He said, "Where is your husband?"

I said, "In the jail in Atlanta, Georgia."

He asked, "Have you got any kids?"

I said, "Yeah, two."

I showed him my sisters' pictures, Judy and Ann's pictures, because they were little at the time. So I didn't know if I'd ever see him again or not. He kept coming back whenever I decided I'd stayed in Everglades long enough. I went back home to Georgia as our parents were living in Georgia then. That was 1935. Aunt Lois wanted Ann to stay with her, so she stayed the full twelve years and went to school. While I was at home Harley kept writing and calling. Finally he said, "I'm coming up there." He came and wanted me to come back with him.

I said, "No, no, no. I can't go back with you now because my sister and I bought a living room suite, and I've got to stay here and pay for half of it. Wait 'till I get this living room suite paid up. So I stayed, but made arrangements about when I should come to Florida.

We were going to get married on Christmas Day, 1937. It was during the depression. The reason we decided to get married on Christmas Day was because all the people who lived in Clewiston couldn't afford to take off other holidays as it was depression days, but they could get off on Christmas Day. There was no church in Everglades, but that was all right. I didn't have a bridal gown, anyway. Harley did get me some rings, but I didn't have any flowers.

The preacher had a little parsonage in a little apartment. The preacher's name was Rev. Baughn. We went to his house and got married and came back and had our big Christmas Wedding dinner at Aunt Lois' house, which was the laundry. We all lived in the laundry in Everglades City.

Aunt Lois was an excellent cook. We had turkey and dressing and the usual. All these people that came brought things. They didn't go down to the weddin' because the preacher had such a small place they couldn't get in. After that we moved to Naples. Read more about me and Frances and our Merry-Go-Round store.

RIDING NIGHT PATROL ON THE TRAIL
Harley Chesser

I was born in 1913 in Blake, Florida. That's about half way between Port Orange and Daytona. My father's name was Lonnie Chesser. My mother was Sophronia Metts. In our family we had Mable, Ethel, me, Clyde and Gerald, the youngest. We came to Naples late in 1926. We stayed with Raymond Bennett, a cousin.

In 1934 I was a mounted policeman riding for the night patrol on a Harley Davidson motorcycle on the Tamiami Trail. I ran into two piles of rock on the side of the Trail. I ended up with 298 stitches and 17 broken bones. We had a freeze that night, and I nearly froze. I had a watch that stopped at five minutes 'till six. I was supposed to be back in Ochopee by 6:00. That was the end of my run. My brother-in-law found me about 9:30. I had bled quite a bit.

When the Trail was first opened Mr. Collier had mounted police riding between the stations on the Trail. The first bridges were decked with two by fours. Nineteen thirty-four was the first year they had the American Legion Convention in Miami.

With truck traffic on the Trail the bridges started going bad. They would get holes in them and when the two by fours got broke they would stick out and cause accidents. I had a kerosene lantern with a red shade on the back of my motorcycle. If I found a bad place I'd stick the two by four up in it and hang the red lantern on it. That was my job for two nights; then I had the accident.

It was a miracle I lived.

I'd see panthers, two or three a night, when I was riding patrol. I carried a 22 pistol because owls would be sittin' on those bridge banisters and fly right out at my light. They almost knocked my head off sometimes. I learned if I shot in their direction just before I got to them, they would fly away. You learned a lot of things to save yourself in these wilds. There was a 14-foot alligator lying in the Trail. I used to see black bears along in there. In the five years I worked for the state I made quite a few trips up and down that Trail, and it was primitive then. I knew the McGills who ran the Monroe Station back then, too.

MR. BARRON COLLIER'S CHAUFFEUR
John Briggs, Sr.

I was born in 1910 in Tifton, Georgia. We came to Florida when I was six years old. In 1917 my father worked in the sawmill at old Manasota, also called Woodmere. That was a big, big sawmill. That was a big settlement, too. We lived in nice, modern two-story houses. It was owned by Germain. They paid with something like a checkbook. Each page was a different value of coins. They paid you by the month. If you needed money before payday you could use these pages, but it came out of your next pay if you used them. Don't get them pages if you aren't going to spend it.

My folks moved from Woodmere to Limestone near Arcadia. First I had a job dredging for Mr. Collier in Punta Gorda, around the hotel there. My brother-in-law got me the job in the garage in Everglades working on the motorcycles that ran the Trail.

Back when I came game was so plentiful. I was driving a big transport truck to Miami. Between Monroe and Ochopee I ran into a flock of a hundred turkeys. I couldn't believe there were that many turkeys. I saw lots and lots of deer. There were lots of turkeys between Naples and Royal Palm Hammock, too.

The canals along the Trail were plumb full of alligators.

I came to Naples in 1929. There wasn't nothin' here. There was the Old Naples Hotel. We all looked forward to the old hotel opening up in the season. That put a lot of people to work. We called the girls that followed that hotel business "biscuit shooters."

I rented the Standard Station when I came from Bill Clark. Back in the old part of town there were a few old houses. There was a school. We used to cut Christmas trees where Palm Pharmacy is today.

Mrs. Briggs added: That was our biggest delight – hunting that tree. They only grow in sand.

She went on: Eli ran Club 41. We didn't know his last name. We didn't go by last names.

John spoke up: The bridge over the Gordon River was a narrow wooden bridge. While they were building it we were pumping in the fill. We filled in from the bridge down to Davis Boulevard. That was low, flat land. You could pump all night long. It looked like it was hard ground, but you go out there to walk and you'd go down over your head.

Nothin' much was around here. The liquor store looked like a horse stable with exposed studs. They sold moonshine in there.

When we moved to Naples we rented Andrew Weeks' house in East Naples.

About the first one I met when we moved up to Naples was old man Surrency. He worked on the dredge. That was Merle Harris' father. He was a nice guy. He was in charge of the pipeline crew.

Preston Sawyer was here. Chiz Rivers was here. You couldn't believe nothin' he said. He went barefooted and struck matches on his feet. I knew Jack Prince. Speed Menefee was some guy. He fished on the pier all the time and passed out gardenias to the ladies. A black couple, Ella and George Williams, used to take care of John Pulling.

The woods used to stay full of water all the time. All the water is running off. That hurt this country, but if you are going to develop it you have to do that. Cape Coral was low, flat and full of water and they dug canals. Now it looks a mile high. I've seen water standing knee-deep on the Trail at Belle Meade.

It ain't like it used to be. It seemed to me like when they dug all those canals to build Golden Gate the land began to dry up and we had no more rain. When we had rainy season it was rainy season. It's got to be less and less rain every year. Seems like building canals and draining the land has changed our climate.

Every winter we had to pull people out of the canals. We had people drown in that canal on the Trail. The Glen Samples went in the canal. He got out, she didn't. Somebody got her out. He had on a suit and tie. They were lucky.

Naples – well, if you want to make money, it's better now. If you wanted to enjoy livin,' it was better back in those days.

I was Mr. Barron Collier's chauffeur. Also, I was chauffeur for other important people who came down to Everglades City. Before Barron Collier came there was nothing in Everglades but the Rod & Gun Club. When he came, Everglades became his headquarters for building the Tamiami Trail.

Mrs. Briggs: I want to say my father ran the mess hall. My family was named Johnson. They came from Whitman, Georgia. We lived on Sandfly Pass. My father was brought down here to run the boarding house for the men who were building the Tamiami Trail. He ran that traveling mess hall that you see pictures of during the building of the Trail. "Doc" Johnson of Naples is part of my family. John can talk now.

John said: Florida was really good back then. We really didn't feel the depression so much. Everglades was a close-knit community. Every Saturday night people got together for parties.

During World War II the Coast Guard was served meals for thirty-five cents, and we made money. We served all kinds of food, including turkey. My wife and I cooked there. I was the breakfast cook. It cost fifteen dollars a week, room and board, to stay in the Ivey House, or one dollar a night and thirty-five cents a meal. We had several regular people who came to the Ivey House.

I remember when Governor Dave Sholtz and D. Graham Copeland had a pow wow party for the Indians out on the Trail. The whole point of this was to make peace with the Indians. There was a monument placed on the spot. The Indians didn't go for it. Speaking of Indians, I know some of them liked to drink. I used to go around with several of the Indians. Jose Billie and Billy Bowlegs I knew well. Billy Bowlegs was always out gar fishing. The Indians roasted them without cleaning them the way we do. He told me roasting them the way they did seasoned them. Deaconess Bedell lived right up the street from us. Indians were always at her house. Deaconess did an awful lot to bring the Indians into civilization.

My sister ran the Ivey Boarding House in Everglades. It was called The Fry House. It is still there. Several of the young Indians would go out and kill young frying turkey and sell them to my sister to serve at the boarding house.

When we had storms in Everglades City we had to almost swim to get back to our houses.

John, Jr. entered the conversation: Dad, remember after hurricanes us kids used to float down the streets in washtubs? Powerboats actually went down the streets, too. My mother reminds us today that if anybody mentions storm everybody here gets scared to death. Well, when we were kids we could hardly wait for a storm so we could get out and paddle around in the storm water.

John, Sr. answered: Yes, I remember, son. I'll tell you about Barron Collier. He was a good fellow and nice looking. He paid for our doctor when we needed medical care. If the doctor in Everglades couldn't take care of you, he would send you to a specialist in Miami. It was just like working for your daddy. We all looked up to him.

Mrs. Briggs chimed in: When we got married we didn't have a dime to our name. Mr. Collier sent Judge Jolley over to Miami with us to pick out a whole house full of furniture. We appreciated having work, and we were to always buy our supplies from his store. The depression was coming on and even his money tightened up during that. I think it was because he bought fifteen of the biggest hotels in the state of Florida and lost some of them. That was the middle '30s. After that he sort of put Everglades on its own.

John, Sr. continued: If you did good work for Mr. Collier you would never get fired. You would get paid more money than you could anywhere else. Once I went to pick up Mr. Collier's luggage to take it to Boca Grande. I was to meet him there. I overslept and I was late getting to Boca Grande, so I missed Mr. Collier and his guests by fifteen or twenty minutes. They were on their way to Useppa Island. Mr. Collier owned that island. He had several big yachts that he used to get along the Gulf waters. I took the luggage to the train depot in Murdock. The agent stopped the train and put it on the train to Boca Grande.

D. Graham Copeland was a great man, too.

The Collier garage where I worked was over by the City Dock across the river in Everglades City in DuPont. There were lots of old locomotive trains. Some of them were very old. They were antiques, really. Mr. Collier had a large collection in a huge warehouse. He liked things like that. There was all kinds of things in that huge warehouse. There were even piles of Goodyear tires. If some company couldn't pay, he took in goods for payment. He also had a building full of antique cars.

During those years Everglades City was a busy, thriving city. There were more people in Everglades City than there were in Naples in those days. There was no causeway to Chokoloskee.

Mrs. Briggs added: When I started to school I was four years old and I rode the school boat to Everglades City to school. We lived at Sandfly Pass. He had an idea for vegetable juice, something like V-8 juice. He needed workers for that. It didn't last too long, and then orange groves were put in. That was in the early 1920s. About one hundred acres died because the men in charge didn't understand how to care for them.

John, Jr. said: When I was just a young kid in Everglades City, I remember being at my Uncle Earl Ivey's boarding house. They had the Coast Guard down there during the war staying at the Ivey Boarding House. I was born in the second house down from the Ivey House. The man who owned the Carr Hotel came. Also, George Chase and his wife used to come often.

John, Sr., continued his memories: Back in the early days we had very few lawmen. During prohibition I remember Chief Hutto was shot by bootleggers on the Everglades dock. The county usually just had a chief of police and a deputy in Everglades. Those days there weren't six hundred people in the whole county.

When Collier finished the Trail he put on five mounted police on motorcycles. He built a filling station for them to live in. Their duties were from Belle Meade to the Dade County line. These policemen were to patrol the Trail to help people in trouble.

One reason I went to Everglades was to work on the motorcycles for Collier, as well as other motors in his garage. Back then everything was run through Everglades because it was the county seat. A newspaper was put out, but nobody read it much. There weren't too many to buy it. At voting time men went round and said, vote for this one or that one.

Mr. D. Graham Copeland was Mr. Collier's right-hand man.

Mrs. Briggs broke in: You know what Mr. Copeland did for us every Christmas? He would put up a huge Christmas tree. There were a lot of poor people down there and he saw that everybody got a present. Also, everybody that worked for him got a turkey or a ham. It's no wonder the town of Copeland was named for him.

THE MAN WITH A PLAN
L.L. Hampton

Being a citizen of Collier County since December 1927, there are a few things that I know of and have seen, that may be of interest to someone that I could tell. The first trip to Naples, where I was transferred by the State Road Department (now named D.O.T.) from Punta Gorda, Florida, the roads were paved all the way to the North Collier county line. From that point on to Naples the road was twin ruts, each about 30' wide of oyster shell. In most instances you had to stop in order to pass approaching traffic. However, there was very little traffic, and many times when you would not meet anyone, between Naples and Bonita Springs.

In arriving in Naples my first thing to do was to meet the people I was to work with and find a place to live. Robert Wilson, Project Engineer with the S.R.D. (Plumb Bob) was contacted, recently transferred from Everglades City to the Naples area, and met the S.R.D. crew.

I don't remember where I spent my first night in Naples, but I think it was at the Bayshore Inn, (it has been torn down) located on the Back Bay. This building was a two-story wooden frame structure with a stairway to second floor where it afforded several small sleeping rooms, screened windows, and a screen door for each room. We had electricity, but the problem was the fact that the plant was shut down at 12:00 P.M. and not started up again until next morning.

Downstairs on the ground floor on the past side Mr. Mac Tolby operated a restaurant, which made it convenient in obtaining meals, and adjacent to and east of the restaurant was general store operated by Mr. Davis. The office and headquarters for the S.R.D. was located on the second floor, in the northeast corner, of Bowling Brothers General Merchandise Store. This frame building still stands, and is in use at Third Street South. The room upstairs, adjacent to and east of S.R.D. office housed a telephone office (now Wind In The Willows) equipment with an ole' fashioned switch board, maybe about forty plug-in, connected with Ft. Myers, Florida, operated by one operator. The balance of the second floor space was occupied by SAL holders of considerable property in Naples at that time and sponsored by Mr. Warfield.

Our work to start with was the Tamiami Trail east of Naples Bay to Palm Hammock, and as I remember the S.R.D. project numbers were 669Y and 669X. The contractor was Alexander, Ramsey and Kerr, who was building the grade for the road. The contractors' superintendent that I knew personally and was acquainted with was young Barron Collier, a nephew of the founder of Collier County.

The trail from Naples to Everglades was not complete, unsuitable for travel, and it was very difficult to drive from Naples to Everglades City. Marco was accessible only by boat and A.C.L. railroad. The only way was to use a ferry to get your car on the island, and it was very limited in capacity.

In returning to Naples W. R. Wilson and I formed an Engineering and Land Surveying firm in 1953 named Wilson & Hampton. At that time, to the best of my knowledge, there were only three registered engineers listed in Collier County: W.R. Wilson, Harmon Turner and myself. Having formed an engineering firm, we attended most of the County Commissioners meetings

In the late '20s I personally saw water flow across Tamiami Trail to Belle Meade area as well as several miles that was under water between Naples and Ft. Myers. In some cases it was deep enough to drown out automobiles. This flooded condition required staking the edge of the road.

Floodwaters flowed across the Tamiami Trail during the storm "Donna" in the East Naples area I would like to point out that to the best of my remembrance the highest recorded rainfall in this area is 120 inches, ranging to approximately 35 inches per annum.

LITTLE SNAKE HUNTER OF THE EVERGLADES
Robert Bruce Warren

When I was just a kid, long before I moved out in the Everglades to live, I came out there to hunt snakes. There was a snake farm outside of Miami, and we kids used to sell them to the snake farm. Also, Ross Allen in Silver Springs and Bill Haas bought them during the years when we kids came out to hunt snakes on Tamiami Trail. We'd stop at those culverts and pick dozens of water snakes at one stop. We caught them by hand. Sometimes if you messed up they'd chew on you a little and brought a little blood. You would just pick off the fangs and forget it. My God, the cottonmouths were everywhere. Of course we had to pin them to pick them up. We also caught frogs, turtles, 'coons or anything we could catch. We hunted snakes at night on the Trail.

We went to Lake Okachobee and got the yellow rat snakes out of the pump houses. We got indigo snakes around Homestead, which were legal to hunt at that time. We, as little kids, hiked on the Trail to the Everglades from Miami to snake hunt. We got tired and would just lay down on the Trail and sleep. No cars came along much in those days. We used a pillowcase to put the snakes in.

Once, when we got a ride to go home our pillow case was moving and the man asked, "What is in your sack, boys?" When we answered, "snakes," he put us out. After that we put them in a tighter bag and squeezed the top down close to the snakes. If anybody asked us what we had we said, "It's our lunch." We caught snakes for years and sold them to the Serpentarium and other places for $.05 an inch.

My older brother, Rhea, was a snake hunter, too, when he was younger. He ended up being connected to the county zoo. He went on to college, became well known in his field.

My brother, Rhea, even took John Kennedy, Jr. out snake hunting once on Loop Road. On another trip he took Julie Nixon Eisenhower out hunting in the Everglades.

The kids in our family are unique. My sister, Carol married a game warden. She worked in the Ochopee Post Office awhile. My brother, John was a 'gator poacher. I was a swamp bum and the other brother, Rhea, is a scientist.

There was a still back in the woods on the Trail. It was on a little island. I was younger than the other guys who were really involved in it. I was the lookout for them. A bunch of Indians found the still and were all drunked up on the island. At the still they made white lightening and the Indians were full of it. Sometimes you could sell to Indians and sometimes not. It depended which politician was in power and the rules he made.

Eddie Hawkins, Sr. owned Glader Park. Eddie, Jr. was in the service several years then came back. He and his wife built a little house next to Eddie, Sr.'s store on Loop Road. Eddie came back with a beautiful wife who was as out of place there on Loop Road as Queen Victoria would be with a bunch of bums and that is what we were on Loop Road. A lot of people looked down on us as swamp rats.

One night Eddie's wife said to me, "I've never told anyone here this, but I am the great, great granddaughter of Ralph Waldo Emerson. Here she was living on Loop Road. Of all people to be living out there where there weren't twenty people living within fifty miles, she was on Loop Road ten or twelve years.

I ended up on Loop Road at Forty-Mile Bend and the Trail at Monroe Station which was one terminus of Loop Road. In the early 1970s there was an old man that worked at Trail Center that I got to be close friends with. I was a sixteen-year-old kid, and this man was in his fifties. He was Bennie Blitch. He just sat around in the woods and drank beer and worked here and there and collected his government check. He was a fascinating old character. This was about the time the government was getting interested in the Big Cypress. I told him that I thought it would be a good idea if somebody could write about the people out there and the life they lived because it was bound to change if it all became Big Cypress. That old man spent two years doing it, but he was the one that really got the National Geographic Society out there to write about the life in the Everglades.

When Mrs. Caulfield came from National Geographic they wanted my picture and story. I sent them to Bill Sholaman. I'm glad I instigated it. I suppose my father's influence comes out in me sometimes.

There were some interesting characters living on Loop Road then. Irvin Rouse, an old country boy from Georgia sat around drinking beer. He wrote the song, Orange Blossom Special years before he came to Everglades. He sang it all the time in 'Gator Hook Bar. Johnny Cash did that song later. Irvin got mentioned in the National Geographic and I thought that was terrific. I used to own the land the Gator Hook Bar was on. I gave it to Jack Knight who bought the bar on the property. My whole life was out there for more than fifteen years on that Loop Road. You have no idea what life was like out there unless you've lived it.

When I lived with Bill Bennett I pumped gas at Trail Center. When I worked at Glader Park I took care of the airboats and bailed them out. Back then it wasn't anything for frogers to go out and get three or four hundred pounds of frogs in a night. Another thing that needs to be addressed today is the diminishing wild life in the Everglades.

I love the Everglades. When I was just a kid I used to track 'coons on the Deering estate, now the county park. I went to Loop Road to track 'coons for a number of years. After I moved to the Everglades I worked at Trail Center that was called George Hunter's place. It was where three counties Dade, Monroe and Collier join. I said I moved in with Bill Bennett who lived back in the woods. He was an old man in his sixties or seventies who was half blind. He lived in a chickee across from an old Indian, named Harry Outlaw. The camp where Harry Outlaw lived in this area, is part of Midway. Bill Bennett was kin to Bennetts who surveyed in the 1800s. From there I went to live in Glader Park near Coopertown. At Glader Park the huntin' season was the time everything went on out in the Everglades. There would be droves of hunters with their airboats, swamp buggies and even airplanes. They needed supplies, and they came into the little store on Loop Road and to Pine Crest Lodge.

I moved from Glader Park to Pine Crest Lodge which was owned by Eddie Hawkins in 1956 and 1957. Part of Loop Road was paved once, but it had deep potholes. We had no electricity and no telephone for miles. We had a generator. We had to buy everything retail. We couldn't buy wholesale. We had no license, so we went to Miami to buy twenty cases of beer for the hunters, thirty pounds of hot dogs or ham. We had to haul our diesel fuel for the generator too. We sold bait, tackle and sandwiches. We had a pool table and a jukebox. There were no places to stay but there were hunting camps back in the woods. A lot of these guys in Miami used to use hunting as an excuse to get away from their wives and play out in Pine Crest. We'd be open until two or three in the morning. Sometimes when I went to bed I could hear those airboats going out to camps. They would be sitting around in those camps waiting for the hunting season to open at daylight. During that time they would drink up all the beer and they would use another twenty gallons of gas for the airboat to come back in for more beer to last until morning. By the time morning came some of them were too drunk or hung over to go hunting. Some though, were serious hunters. There was Old Ben Hess out there with them.

Right on Loop Road two airboats ran together and two people were killed coming around blind curves. Back then there were no guards on the props. Most airboats didn't have starters, so you had to stand up there and pull the prop over to crank the engine. The bottom of the boat was always slippery from oil leaking out of the engine. For steering, some guys just had a wire going back to the carburetor. Those first airboats were dangerous.

During the hunting season or when some people came out from Miami to the bar, there would naturally sometimes be trouble. There was absolutely no law out in Pinecrest. Somebody might have too much to drink, argue over a pool game or something somebody said about one of the wives. Once, during an argument at that exact time somebody pulled the trigger on a gun, a girl out front fainted. Somebody thought she was shot and she was carried in and put on the pool table. It scared me so much I had to do something. I had an old beat up car with no tag and four tires of different sizes, but I drove to Miami and got on a bus and went all the way to Key West to the county seat to talk to the sheriff, as we were in Monroe County and Key West was the county seat. I asked if he could some way get some law in Pine Crest. Dade and Collier law ignored it as it wasn't in their counties. Key West was too far away.

Early on most of the little settlements around Miami sprang up around a bar and some were rough. You could get killed in one. A lot of people were afraid of Pine Crest. Nobody needed to be afraid. Sometimes a car wouldn't come down the road for days. It was safe out on Loop Road.

My father was campaign manager for Spessard Holland twice when he ran for Governor of Florida. He was later the senator in Washington, D.C. I called on him to help me get mail delivery out on the Trail to the people of our Pine Crest area. In those days the mail was being left at Monroe Station and stuck behind the register until the people happened to come in. Several of the retired people out there weren't getting their Social Security checks until a week later or more. I felt bad about this so I went to the Indian Village and I went to the phone about 6:00 one night. I got on the phone and said, "I am Robert Warren, and I want to call Senator Spessard Holland in Washington, D.C." He picked up the phone, believe it or not.

I said, "You don't know me from Adam, but my father, Cecil Warren was your campaign manager." I told him I wanted to do something about getting mail delivered to these people up and down this Trail out here. That was in the 1960s. He told me to write all the particulars to him and he would see what he could do.

These people out there didn't know anything about my background or who my family was. I was just a swamp bum to them. I was just one of the crowd. I was just "little old Bruce, the snake hunter kid." About three months later bump, bump down Loop Road came a guy in a brand new car. He walked in and says, "I'm from the Post Office Department in Tampa." I took him and showed him all the junk trailers everybody lived in and the rundown bars and shacks. He said, "Well, we will see what we can do. About three months later there was a mail route out of the Ochopee Post Office to Pine Crest. Before that, people in Loop Road had to go to Ochopee, the closest Post Office which was fifty miles away. Monroe, Collier and Dade Counties came together and those three counties join and receive mail from the Ochopee Post Office. Most of those people didn't have any way to get to Ochopee in those days.

I instigated getting The *National Geographic* people down here, too. I didn't want the story on me. I sent them to do one on "Gator Bill. I'm not as proud of getting the mail route out there as I am of getting The National Geographic people out there to do a story on the Everglades and its people and leaving me out of it. I felt if I put myself in it, then I wasn't doing something unselfishly. I think the greatest thing in the world is to give to people and not let them know where it come from.

I lived right down from the Ochopee Post Office. I bought a house from Forest Harmon. By that time I was doing surveying.

I left out of there then and went to Turner Road. That's where I met my wife. She is from Everglades. Pine Crest was still primitive in those days. We who lived out there had a time making a living. My brother, John, skinned alligators. I hunted snakes and worked in a bar and worked at whatever I could.

The more assets a man has the more damage he can do to the environment. We didn't have any assets. The Federal Government, with unlimited assets has done more to damage the Everglades than can be measured. Private interests and developers have done more damage to Florida than the working man. It's the "big" people who destroy the world's environment, not the little people.

One day I saw these surveyors going up and down Loop Road. I didn't have any money, so I begged them for a job. There was an old man in his sixties named George Tomlinson. He was born on Marco Island. I was put with him to start chaining out in the cypress strand. We were doing all of

Pine Crest. I liked working outdoors and doing surveying. The jetport was only about fifteen miles from Pine Crest, and so I got work surveying at the jetport.

There was a big controversy going on about the jetport. President Jimmy Carter sent Joe Browder to do something about the controversy. In 1960 there were strange feelings in this whole country during those years. In these days people have no integrity. All they have is greed.

I'll never forget the first day I went out with George Tomlinson. We were chaining in water up to our waists. A storm came up, and he said, "Drop the chain. It's lightening." About that time it struck somewhere and he got shocked. He went up in the air and did about three flips in the air, and landed on his feet and says, "Let's go home."

I love that country called the Everglades. I love it with all my heart, and want to do something to preserve it. My whole life has been involved in this project. That is why I've been trying all these years to get the Tamiami Trail designated a historical highway. At last it seems like it will happen. That will be the happiest day of my life.

Once I read an article that Pine Crest subdivision was laid out as a logging camp originally. It had a couple of little stores and a schoolhouse during the first Pine Crest settlement. The Purple Gang out of Chicago with Dutch Schultz owned Pine Crest first. This man who I knew was acquainted with Jim Dill very well. Jim Dill was a "bag man" I knew for that gang. This man was in his early twenties and in all the speakeasies around Miami, so he would have known the truth about all this. The article stated that the little town of Pine Crest was a ghost town twice in the same century. It is the only town in Florida that has that distinction. The first time it became a ghost town was because the logging gave out. The second time was after prohibition, during Al Capone's days in Pine Crest. Now it is in the national park.

Jim Dill, a part of Al Capone's gang, was a retired captain of the Spanish American War in Cuba in 1898. There was a gambling place right in that piney wood called Pine Crest. People were brought in by helicopter to gamble. The only road out there was the one to Immokalee. Remember Key West was the county seat, and it was too far away. Dade or Collier had no jurisdiction over Pine Crest.

In 1928 or '29, Al Capone's gambling lodge burned. Jim Dill Road in Pine Crest had three lodges where prominent people from Miami came to gamble.

If something happened you settled it yourself. Jim Dill was very secretive and lived to himself. He had been thrown out of the gang for something so he had come out to Pine Crest to live out his life. He lived to be one hundred.

Let me tell you about that movie, *Wind Across the Everglades*. Cory Osceola was in it. Brad Bradford was in the movie too. I'll insert this story about Brad. He used to buy snakes from us kids. One day he said, "You boys take that 'coon out there back out that Trail with you to the Everglades. He is a nuisance. Well, we found out something. The police stopped us and said it was MGM's movie pet coon and we had to give it back. Bradford was drunk most of the time. Well, Brad Bradford was in that movie. The name was changed from Cotton Mouth, to Wind Across the Everglades. He showed me the script before it ever came out. Burl Ives, Christopher Plummer, Gypsy Rose Lee, they were in Everglades for it. Budd Schulberg was the producer from Warner Brothers. They had Everglades all put up with these false storefronts. If you went behind them, two by fours were holding them up. I've never seen a movie set before. Brad was the curator, taking care of the movie animals. We kids sold him a bunch of snakes for it. It tickled me because the only snake I remember seeing in the movie was a dead banded water snake that Brad gave to Burl Ives to shake around to make it look alive. Totch Brown was in the movie too.

Here are some of the little things I remember about living on Loop Road. Old Negro George lived on the left-hand side of the Trail about one mile west of Monroe Station. He let men from Miami leave their swamp buggies at his place. Someone burned him out. It was a shame.

I remember when my friend, Daryl Gay, used to walk up and down the trail with his finger in a Pepsi bottle and a pillowcase over his shoulder when we were hunting for snakes.

The original swamp marker was found burned. But the Governor said the new survey stood. I remember Brownell's claim was that the three county lines for Dade, Monroe and Collier were in the wrong place. When I worked at Glades Park one gas pump was in one county and one in another.

Benny Blitch said this to a man who griped about all the water around Pine Crest, "If you don't like water what are you doing living in the Everglades? One thing, this trail is open at both ends."

Rails from the train that hauled logs out of the woods are under Scenic Drive. Pine Crest was like the last frontier. No law - totally free - no taxes. People in New York or somewhere east might own land in Pine Crest, but they didn't care what took place, as they never came.

I remember when water was bumper deep in the rainy season. You pushed water as you went.

Monroe Station had the "tree with a hole in it." The huge tree in front was cut away for power lines.

In the 1960s, a big fire came through and burned my chickee of fourteen hundred palms, my gas stove, refrigerator, and everything I had. All I could do was stand and watch it burn. Afterward, I helped fight fires for others.

I remember Indian Harry Outlaw moved when the lake and trail was built. Everything new has no atmosphere. Old buildings like Monroe Station never lose their atmosphere.

I remember Charley Tiger took us back to an Indian snake dance. It was a fire water party.

I remember Daryl's hogs on Jim Dill Road. Some guy fed mash to his hogs. They were drunk all the time.

John Cooper built the first air boat in Cooperstown.

Pine Crest was a real hide away for some and it was a sportsman's paradise. "There were twenty-two acres of marijuana inside the loop. It was burned.

In the old Pine Crest, a Black raped a White woman and they hung 21 blacks that night. Black town was bought. The Blacks made whiskey with wheat, beans, and sugar, with lye added.

Ed Hawkins and nine other men started the Air Boat Association in 1952. It was started to fight the game commission because they were trying to stop us from hunting frogs and hogs. Nobody cared about ecology until the 1960s.

I remember I picked up a tiny wild pig one time. I had a boxer dog with a false pregnancy. That dog raised that pig until that pig was bigger than she was.

I dearly loved my life in the Everglades. What I want to do is get people to take notice and made a conscious decision. There are so many historic things that get destroyed because nobody takes the time to make a conscious decision and it all disappears. Monument Circle is an example. I had no idea until twenty years later that my father was responsible for that after it deteriorated.

A guy told me Jim Dill burned Al Capone's lodge down. Ducky had been around those early private clubs before prohibition. He knew Jim Dill well.

During Hurricane Donna in 1960, Eddie and I stayed in that store. We started puttin' plumbin' strap up as the roof was given in. We left and went down to the chicken ranch. They had a C. B. buildin'. There was me and Freddie Danhoff, Eddie Hawkins and Ethel and Sandy. That was the little concrete place Dewe lived in. After the storm, when we went back to the store, we saw the sixteen-penny nails were pulled out halfway. That's how near the roof came to blowin' off. The mornin' after Donna, the wind was still blowin' 60 or 70 miles an hour. I headed down the Loop Road and there were white caps goin' across Loop Road. I drove out on the Trail toward Everglades City and every second pine tree was layin' across the road. I came back and got an ax to cut my way through. There were some Indian boys tryin' to get toward Miami. They had cut quite a few. I managed to get to Everglades City that day. On that curve that goes to Chokoloskee, Donna took the pavement and laid it out in rows on top of the lime rock. I must say this about my older brother. Back in 1968, Rhea went to Komoda Island with the National Geographic to study these flesh eating lizards, the Komoda dragons.

MY DAYS ON THE TRAIL
Lowell Goldie

My grandfather, Hugh Joseph Goldie, was born in Scotland. Everybody called him "Scotty." He stowed away when he was about 15 years old. The old captain on the ship that he was on found him after they were three days out. It was too far to take him back. He liked the boy and called him "Scotty." The old captain raised my granddaddy.

My daddy worked with Granddaddy Goldie on the ships for a while. That's the way my folks came up. Later, when he was at Burnham Clam Factory on Marco, they sailed to Key West for supplies. He sailed a boat named Blue Heaven, too. He ran the Burnham Clam factory in Caxambas when Preston Sawyer was a boy living there. I don't know how or when Granddaddy came to Ft. Myers, but he met Grandma there. Her name was Ella Rylander. She was from New Orleans. Her family was one of the first settlers in Estero.

My father was Hugh Martin Goldie. There were a lot of kids in my family. There was Stanley Dale, which we called "Rat;" Gerald Wayne, Clinton (we called him "Skinny"); then there was Eldon that we called "Bud." Next was Shelly, Velma and Aliene.

After Wanda and I got married we owned two lots on the property where the telephone company is now on Davis Boulevard. Junior and his family lived nearby. Wanda and I have lived in Myrtle Cove 25 years. We have been married 40 years.

We worked lots of prisoners. When I worked on the Tamiami Trail for 26 years I'd leave every morning early, and Wanda could hear my truck cross ever' bridge. We lived on Davis Boulevard in a tarpaper house. There weren't much traffic on the Trail back then. There were horrible wrecks on Cypress Bend. They were caused most by the old bridges. I'd happen along and try to help. Lots of people got killed on the Trail. One bad wreck I remember was one mornin' as I went to work. I stopped in time to see a woman having her baby. The other little kids were in the car with her. She was yelling, "Please help my husband." He was throwed out and somehow his head was cut off; his body was there on the bank, and his head had rolled down in the ditch. She and the kids didn't know it. She was havin' that baby.

Finally a man came along in a station wagon. We got her and the baby and the kids in it, and I covered up her husband in the back and the man carried them all to Ft. Myers Hospital. That was the worst one I believe I've ever seen. Drivin' that Trail back in the early days could be treacherous.

We worked out of Everglades City, and when hurricane Donna come we got our equipment and some of our trucks under water. It was a bad storm. It was hard to live them days, but we lived it and had happy times.

MEMORIES OF THE TRAIL
Ed Tompson

There is a story that came from an early settler who was one of the Jaudon men who helped locate Tamiami Trail, J. Frank Jaudon, a Frenchman. He had lived in Miami. He was the second reporter clerk who, in those days, kept the records around 1918 and 1919 in Dade County

J. Frank Jaudon helped lay out the original line for the Tamiami Trail. He was about the second settler to settle in Ochopee. He started a farm on the north side of Turner's River, which is the north side of what is now Tamiami Trail. He lived there part-time and Miami part-time.

He was one of the first farmers to put in fields north of Carnestown. He helped build one of the first packinghouses on the Tamiami Trail. He also became the official acquirer of Florida property in Collier County for Barron Collier. He put a small subdivision near Ochopee (Pinecrest) in 1928, which consisted of about thirty acres of land. That was the first subdivision in that part of the County. I started the survey for the causeway from Everglades City to Chokoloskee.

In the 1930s one of the important items that got my interest: kids of school age graduated from school on Halfway Creek. That school was built sometime in 1920. They had built a walkway from Halfway Creek to the schoolhouse on the north side of Halfway Creek about where the Clere's subdivision now sits. That walkway was built out of conch shells about two feet deep for a couple hundred feet. It went up on a small Indian mound then they cut black, fine timber and put a small building up about four by twelve with four windows in it and two doors. This was still intact in the late 1930s but it got tore up. It was originally called Smith's School. It was named for the family that had settled in that area. There were four or five boys: Wilburn, Ike, Heb and Lee, and some girls, too. The first one married Cecil Toole.

Hilda married J. B. Webb. Mattie, the third one, married somebody from Goodland. There was another group that lived in New Haven. That old school was called Smith School because of all those Smith kids in there. It eventually got torn down by tornadoes, winds, or such, so there is nothing left now, other than just the posts that the floor sat on. The conch-shell walkway is still in there going down through the mangroves.

The people on Chokoloskee decided it was time to get some of their tax money back, so they petitioned to have a road built from Everglades City over the Chokoloskee. Now the grammar grades' kids from Chokoloskee were walking to this Smith School at Halfway Creek. The higher-grade kids were using a boat to go to school. They used Smallwood's Store for a landing on the Chokoloskee side and the back canal for a landing on the mainland. So it fell my lot to do the regular location work under a man by the name of G. W. Butler who was an old-timer with the Florida State Road Department and a registered engineer.

To begin, we started running lines across Chokoloskee Bay. We put in about three or four lines, all of which were turned down because the tide was affecting the area too much that the road was going to be lying in. As the road is, in 1991 is where the final line was put in.

One of the interesting things that took place on that line was I had a man working for me who had lived all his life in the so-called City of Miami. He apparently had never been in the woods to work. We started telling him about these fish that were in Chokoloskee Bay that would bite your toe off if you stepped on one of them. Well that disrupted the whole organization for about a week. This fellow would go along and stick his foot way out in front of him and move it really easy all over the bottom of the bay before he put it down. He'd pick up his other foot, and he'd move it all over the bay in front of him and then put it down. Finally somebody yelled, "Ouch!" That wound him up, and he quit.

In going on to Chokoloskee Island from Everglades City, a few interesting things showed up. Now I had been told years before that some people had died on a ship in the Gulf and had been brought into Chokoloskee Island. They had been very sick with fever. Three of them died. Mr.

Smallwood had them buried a couple of hundred feet from the north end of Chokoloskee. This happened sometime in the late 1920s or early 1930s. I was a little dubious of the facts, but the State Road Department wanted to know about it. Therefore, I went to see Mr. Dan McLeod, who was an abstractor in Everglades City. He had a record of it, all right. They had been buried all those years, and people had forgotten their names. When the road was being excavated so-called human bones were moved.

Right at the north end of Chokoloskee there used to be a three-foot high mound above the water, and it had to be cut down. That's where the Brown Motel place is today. That causeway was dredged, and material was pumped in out of Chokoloskee Bay, parallel with the road. Supposedly there would be a dug canal so people wouldn't have to go across the middle of the Bay.

When the dredgers were two thirds of the way across they started hitting hard shell, and it couldn't be pumped, so the idea was dropped. Now the canal is on the north side of that causeway, but one time it was flanked by mangroves on both sides. Now that is the route that the Everglades Park boats take.

The mosquitoes were a big problem when we were building that road. At one time they got so bad that we couldn't see the sun come up in the morning through our window screens. They'd be solid. At night before we went to bed we would take a big quahog clam shell six or eight inches in diameter and about two inches deep. Most of the time we just put up with it. We used rubbing alcohol on our faces, but not too much or it would blister. They weren't as bad in the daytime as at night.

While I worked on the road I lived in Everglades Inn. Barron Collier owned the hotels at the time, the Inn and the Rod & Gun Club. The building that houses the drug store and the Post Office was what remained of the old Everglades Inn. That is the building that burned down. Across from the Inn was the first bus station in Everglades City. When we finished up the survey of the causeway to Chokoloskee, we were assigned to various surveys in Collier County, which included surveys for the roads that the Collier County Commissioners wanted built.

At that time there were only three people in their Engineering Department. One was Harmon Turner, who was also the engineer for the Collier Company. Another was Mr. Perry, and one Indian. I don't know the Indian's name.

One of the most interesting stories I ever heard came to me from one of the Smallwood girls, Thelma Smallwood. The exact date I cannot establish. The Bank of Homestead was robbed by a pair of robbers. They were supposed to have gotten ten thousand dollars in gold, a four-caret diamond ring, plus miscellaneous papers, etc. One of these men was named Leland Rice, who was half Cherokee Indian. The other was named Tucker. I tried to pin it down that he was from Lee County, but it can't be done. I can't find out where he came from.

These men either got rid of the law officers who were following them, or the officers lost their trail. They wound up west in the 'Glades, very close to what is East Cape Sable. People confuse it as one piece of land. Cape Sable is three pieces of land. They are East Cape, Middle Cape and West. What makes this intriguing is that they showed up again on Chokoloskee Island. How did they get there? That is the mystery. Neither of them knew anything about the 'Glades. No boat was found that they used to get there.

They put in at Smallwood's Store. At that time there was a group of Seminoles camping on every shell mound in the mouth of Turner River. They always camped there every year for three or four days, having a big time and drinking. They would then go on to Smallwood's Store, do their trading, then leave. Nobody would see them again for months and months.

These robbers had a pretty good time, too, with the booze bought from the Indians. Word came that Monroe County had sent a deputy sheriff over to apprehend these robbers. Rice and Tucker stayed on Chokoloskee, and the other two disappeared. This happened in 1926. So Rice went out in Chokoloskee Bay and put up in a fish house that was built out there on pilings.

The sheriff did get to Everglades. The Monroe sheriff met the Everglades City sheriff, who was Louis Thorpe. The Everglades sheriff went out in a boat to arrest him at the fish house. The story goes that he beat on the floor above his head with his pistol butt. Rice leaned over the floor of the fish house and asked, "What do you want?"

The deputy said, "I came to pick you up. They want you in Key West."

Rice said, "Fellow, you are talking to the wrong man in the wrong place. You ain't got no business out here a 'tall. I don't care if you are sheriff. I'm not in Monroe County. You can't arrest me."

It was proved that the county line ran right through the middle of the fish house, and he was sittin' in Monroe County. The old foundation is still there.

Rice finally came back to Chokoloskee a few days later. Tucker had got on a drunk in a boat and headed toward Turner's River mouth to get some more liquor. On his way back across the Bay he got in a wind squall and turned the boat upside down. Somebody on the island saw it, but by the time they got to him he was drowned. They brought him in, and buried him on the east side of Chokoloskee Island, about where the Brown's Motel is.

There was a big shell mount there. All these years he laid in that grave without being disturbed until I came along. Doc Brown who used to own the general grocery store there, wanted a survey job done.

I says, "Doc, it'll cost you a little money."

He said, I can't pay it right now, but I'll let you know when. I ought to have it done."

He notified me later that he had to have it done. I said, "All right. I'll make a deal with you. You ain't got much money, and I got a lot of time. Doc, I understand when they dug up the mound over there that you got Robber Tucker's gold teeth."

He said, "Yeah, I've got 'em, Ed."

I says, "Doc, I'll do the survey job for his teeth."

He said, "All right. I don't know how much longer I'll live, but you keep ever'thing else you get your hands on. You might as well have 'em."

I wound up with Tucker's gold teeth, and part of his jawbone.

Gettin' back to Leland Rice: A man in Everglades City was goin' to make Rice tell him where the gold was hid. He went over the Chokoloskee with a pistol and a couple of other men. They cornered Leland at Smallwood's Store. They said, "We want to know where you hid that gold. We don't want all of it. We want part of it. Tell us and we will leave you alone and let you stay here." Rice wouldn't tell them anything about it.

They went on back to Everglades and came back late the next afternoon. Two of the men had shotguns. The first man that had approached him to begin with said, "Rice, we might as well get this settled. Either give us our share of that money, or we will shoot you and get the reward."

Rice said, "Well, fire away." This man did, and shot Rice in the back and killed him standing right by Smallwood's store.

Alvin Williams was one of the residents of Everglades that lived on the west side of Barron River. One of the men had a still set up out on the Tamiami Trial. Alvin would go out and sit on the bridge rail with a 22 rifle in case the law came by and stopped. If they did stop, he'd start shootin' snakes in the river. That was a signal to the man runnin' the still. When he heard those shots he put the fire out. This moonshiner on Turner's River had four kids that he put through high school moonshinin.' I kept wonderin' what happened to him. I know every inch on Chokoloskee Island. Margarete Williams, Mr. Smallwood's daughter, told me she went to the funeral of Leland Rice, and he was buried by a big gumbo limbo tree about twenty-five or thirty feet away from the old school cistern, which was right in the center of the island. I said, "That don't tell me what I want to know. Where was it?"

She said, "I was eleven years old, and I stood right there and watched him be buried in the ground."

The center was the third oldest Church of God church in the southern group of states. That church was established in 1896. I believe I'm right. The Ernest Hamilton family and some of the Smallwoods - - the biggest part of the House boys' wives, were very religious people.

In 1953 or '54 there was a preacher who was a soft-spoken boy until somebody called him a liar. Then he was hard to get along with, and he took it out on the congregation. It took Joe Lopez, an old-timer there. That's a story, too. His father was supposed to have jumped ship out in the Gulf of Mexico, came in the Chokoloskee and then settled on Lopez River. He built a fresh water cistern there. After using the cistern for forty or fifty years he found out there was a small lake there with a spring right in the middle of it. It's still there, too. Salt water all around, but a fresh water spring right in the middle of that lake. I've drank out of it. Good water.

Anyhow, that preacher, Welch, came to me and said, "The church plate hasn't been getting' any money in a long time." He said they wanted to put an addition on the church, and would I do a survey for 'em.

He said, "We don't know when we can pay for it. Maybe we can —maybe we can't."

I said, "I'll do it for you."

They put an addition of some twenty-five or thirty feet on the church. I went on about my business and forgot about it. In about 1973 one of 'em gave me a check for the survey - - thirteen years later. I did a lot of work over there like that. If you get a check, okay; if you don't—forget it. They are good people. I know about a lot of things, but I don't say nothin'—uh-uh.

This is a good one about Everglades City. Our crew was livin' at the Everglades Inn, along with G. W. Butler. Word got out at that a boat was goin' to be in sometime between that afternoon and the next mornin' with a load of rum. Now the Everglades Inn (the building that burned) had a balcony that ran around two sides of it. Everybody sat on the balcony the rest of the afternoon and until late that night waitin' to see that boat come in. Well it got there but it was in the wee hours of the mornin' and ever'body was in bed.

Louis Thorpe, the sheriff, and his two deputies were there. The people on the boat didn't load it until later afternoon. When they got two or three Model-A truck - - flatbeds, they unloaded that stuff and hauled it to two boxcars on the railroad. They had about a third of a boxcar full when they got it loaded. I found out then what "ears" were. Back in those days whiskey came from the islands in bags, and they called them "ears." These bags were smaller than croaker sacks. There was six quarts of whiskey to the bag. When the sewed the sack tops they left some sticking up, and they called those "ears."

They got two rail cars backed off, and they pulled out of Everglades City headed north to Deep Lake. Nobody knew what was taking place on the railroad track. The next day the revenue men got on the train. They were huntin' the whiskey, and finally found one car had been left off on a side track in Deep Lake. The found the second one four or five days later in Jacksonville, Florida. It had made it that far on its way to Chicago or somewhere before being found.

The "revenoors" hired a bunch of blacks who lived in Copeland for the Lee Cypress Corporation to destroy the stuff. Instead, they took some planks and laid them from the boxcar door out to the edge of the road. These people that they hired would get an ear in each hand and carry two sacks of liquor. There was a line of big rocks all the way down #29, so as they went between the rocks, they'd bust one bag between the rocks and throw the other one in the canal. That's the way the one in Deep Lake was unloaded.

Finally somebody called Louis Thorpe up a week later and said, "Louis, you've got to come up here. Everybody's drunk and stayin' drunk, and we don't know where they are getting' the booze."

Thorpe went up there to see what was goin' on. He found out these guys that had throwed it in the canal and were diving it up. They never found any whiskey in the boxcar n Jacksonville. It got unloaded before they got there.

In 1933 or '34 we went to Sam Jones's store. From Ochopee you go on east toward Miami to Monroe Station, turn north and there is a big strand that runs north and south. It goes all the way across Alligator Alley. That's how long it is. We went through the woods to get to the store, but there is an easier way now. You go to the Seminole Indian Reservation north of the Alley and go to County Line Point where three counties come together. Collier, Palm Beach County and Broward County.

Then at the big marker go due south about six or eight miles to this store. This store used to be called Sam Jones Fort site, but it never was a fort. It was always a trading post.

When you talk about Sam Jones, you are getting back to the blacks with the Seminoles. He was an "innerbreed." The old site was one of the main points of intersection during the wars. It was on the main points of intersection of so-called roads. They weren't roads. They were trails that were used during the second and third Seminole wars. Those took place from about 1845 to 1851 or '52.

In 1978 a small group of people from Lauderdale got some financing together and went from East Bay Canal to the fort site. They stayed out there a week and dug up about everything that could be found. I was told metal detectors were used. They found jacket buttons, old pistols, and old wagon hubs, but no money.

Johnny Billie, who is Chief Ingraham's so-called son, came in to my camp one day at Turner's River and said, "I need a shirt," so I gave him a brown work shirt. He walked off without a word. About two weeks later, just before Christmas of 1960 or '61, when Johnny Billie came back with Mary Billie, a member of the clan, they had a brown paper bag. They set it on the chair and handed my shirt back. I looked at the bag and said, "What's that?"

Johnny said, "You see." I opened it up, and there was this beautiful Indian jacket. It is not made out of cotton. It has never been bug-eaten. It is an unusual material. It is colorfast. It has never faded. It is Indian trade cloth called red cotton. I still have it, and I'd still like to know the meaning of the symbols.

I was workin' with this same state survey crew in the early part of 1950. We were locating a reintersection of the Tamiami Trail that turns into Everglades City. Somebody looked up #29 toward Deep Lake, and here came an old Chevrolet flatbed just stacked with Indians. This truck was barely movin' along. We had an Indian boy workin' with us. He was one of the Osceola boys from Ft. Myers. When that old truck crossed the Trail, the Osceola boy started laughin' and clappin' his hands as he stood right in the middle of the road. He kept on laughin' and clappin' his hands.

Mr. Butler asked, "What are you laughin' at? You are Seminole."

He looked Mr. Butler straight in the face and said, "Me no Seminole—me Cow Creek." Now that goes to show you that there are those who know where their families come from even though they are second generation.

Here in Collier County, Ingraham Billie had a camp at Monroe Station. His second camp was at Turner's River, down by Ochopee. Then there was a little difficulty. The Billie tribe and one other tribe on the Trail saw fit to disagree over some matter. Ingraham moved his camp to the Big Cypress Reservation, and that is where he lived until he died in about 1986. I went to see him just before he died. He was one hundred two years old. He has a brother still living.

Jose Billie died before Ingraham. He was one hundred sixteen or so when he died. Ingraham's brother in the Reservation is one hundred fourteen years old. At one time Jose Billie stayed out here north of Turner's River Road. Jose Billie was buried in the swamps.

We have an Indian boy at Palm Hammock that has four kids. They went to school every day in that camp. They spent six hours a day, five days a week, sittin' out under a tree learnin' all there is to know about their race of people; also, how to speak English, and how to act around people. This is what happened to those Miccosukee Indians. One of the teachers in the public schools of Collier County got an injunction to go out there and make them Indian kids come to school in Naples. Their father told the teacher, "Try and do it, and we will move out of the state of Florida."

I'm told that the Indian Commissioner of the Bureau of Indian Affairs in Washington, D.C., said, "Now, just a minute. You aren't going to go out there and take charge of these people. We are glad that you brought it up. We will take charge. The government furnishes the teacher, and what they need."

THE FROG HUNTER
Daryl Gay

Everybody out here on the Trail is different. Don Sullivan owned the barbecue place. He came from Homestead. He was born of one of the old families out of Homestead. He had a place out in the woods where he raised hogs. He was called "Walkin' John." His boat broke down once and he walked in, so he was called "Walkin' John" after that.

In 1960 Hurricane Donna was bad, but the only damage I got was from fire. I figured it this way, a hurricane has to cross a hundred miles of land to get to us here. The wind goes right over us here because the woods is so thick. We had a tornado that did come across here. My wife's brother was out in the yard and I was in the shop. It sounded like a freight train. It jumped and went to hit the Chicken Ranch. It took T. J.'s roof right off and strewed it all around. It took a week to get to Miami. Those Australian pines were like cardboard down through there on the Trail.

Everybody in my business of frogging looked forward to storms. The frogers benefit by the big storm of Donna. I could put it this way, we could frog five percent of the country, but the water has got to come up in the rest of the country to move them frogs. This year the water didn't come up here and 35 pounds was my best night. We didn't have no water to move 'em. It was bad.

Livin' out here in the Everglades is easy goin,' all laid back. We don't press for time. It is a beautiful way of life. If anybody ever came and stayed a few days they never would want to go back. I took my brother out on Loop Road and he stayed out there about fifteen years.

Monroe Station, about 20 miles east of Carnestown, was one of six way stops along the Trail. The resident patrolman drove back and forth on his motorcycle looking for automobiles in trouble with flat tires or breakdowns. His wife stayed at the station pumping gas and serving light refreshments. Monroe Station became a popular restaurant after the Collier interests sold it. It burnt down in 2016.

THE INDIANS OF MONROE STATION I KNEW
Keith King

Buffalo Tiger was the chairman of the tribe. I used to kid him and say, "Billy, someday you will have Buffalo's job." I got acquainted with Jimmy Tiger's son, Charley. He was explaining the reason for the corn dance. He said, "Someday I kill you."

I said, "Charley, we are friends."

One time Billy invited us to a green corn dance. White people aren't supposed to go. They danced around fire and cooked corn.

They have pins in a board and they scratch adults and little kids arms. The little kids would bleed and adults, too.

I asked Billie, "What is that for?"

He would say, It's to let the bad blood out." He said, "No, no. Someday we get back Florida."

Once we went to a Green Corn Dance. It was rough traveling in the Everglades to the spot where they were meeting. We got there a little after dusk. There were fires burning. An old Indian came to our car and looked in. He said, "Old white people – we scalp 'em."

My wife got scared and said we better go back. I took two cases of beer out of my trunk and set them right under the feet of the person in charge. They had several games that night. Old John Osceola made these stick ball bats. The young men catch the ball, throw it over their heads to try to hit a pole. The young women could use their hands to throw the ball over. The young John Osceola said, "We call them La Finenda gloves. Old John gave them to my wife's sister."

Old John Osceola had a daughter named Irene. His wife's name was Mattie.

Probably the best twenty years of my life was spent on the Trail. This plaque was presented which reads:

"May it be known that Keith King and family through their participation with the Micasuki Tribe of Indians of Florida has earned this expression of appreciation for courtesies extended to the tribe. Signified herewith by this Certificate. Signed Billy Cypress, Head of Micasuki Tribe."

Billy Cypress was just a little kid. He lived across from Monroe Station. We hired him to work at our service station. We moved to Trail Center and he moved up there.

We went to the Trail September 1st, 1960. Donna hurricane came the 10th. We were at Monroe Station. Our daughter was visiting us. We heard on the radio station how the hurricane had hit Monroe Station. Later on that year we bought Glader Park. That is just south of Miami. My partner wanted Glader Park, so I traded for his half interest in Monroe Station. After a year we sold that and moved to Whitehall, Illinois. In eleven months she called and wanted us to buy it back. We did, and was there years, then sold it to Dixie Webb.

Monroe Station used to be known as "The Tree with a Hole in it." That tree sets out in front of the Monroe Station, and the telephone lines go there so they cut a hedge hole in the middle of the tree so the lines would be free. People as far away as Illinois knew Monroe Station as the station as "The Tree with a Hole in it."

Many hunters came to Monroe Station. Also boys hunting snakes. The men who parked their buggies at Monroe Station came every weekend to hunt in the Everglades. In Monroe Station we served breakfast, sandwiches, pie and coffee and beer. We were very busy.

Every March the Conservation Club right behind us had a wild hog barbecue.

Monroe Station had a population of three or four, and during wild hog barbecue the population swelled to fourteen thousand. They even came from Europe. There were lots of car accidents on that Trail everyday.

One day a man was killed right in front of Monroe Station. The Indian girl who worked for us and I were watching this Mr. Thompson. As he went to turn in, a car coming from Naples was going fast. It hit him and threw the car up in the air. He was killed. The impact even knocked his shoes off.

At Monroe Station we had an acre of land. Tourists would come in and see these large numbers of cars parked there and they'd look around and even look up the stairway. They thought we had a gambling house. The reason for all the cars was these people would drive out from Miami to Monroe Station and park their cars. A bus would come and pick them up and take them to the Golden Gates Development to sell them land. That was when it was first being developed. We kept our place so clean that salesmen who came in would ask if they could take their clients into our kitchen. We believed in cleaning the corners first and the middle last. Later, in the 1960s we bought the grocery store in Ochopee from Frances Watson. We were there four years before we sold to the government. It isn't there anymore. It was one-quarter mile west of the little Post Office. It was a mess, and Frank Head said, "I know Ada. She will clean and paint everything."

They widened the Trail in Ochopee, and so the little Post Office had to be moved back. They moved it on a wheelbarrow.

The Gaunt/Brown store in Ochopee brought in more income per square foot than any business anywhere. In the early 1950s I had a letter from Mr. Gaunt wanting to sell me some lots in Ochopee.

At Monroe Station there were so many snake hunters they would hitchhike from Miami with a bag. There were some other kids that come out with a rifle. They were shooting everything, even buildings. While they were out there we slept on the floor because we were afraid those bad boys might shoot through the window. That was unusual. Most of the kids were good kids. They caught snakes to sell to the Serpentarium in Miami.

I must tell you about the wild hog barbecue. We had a good business during that time. We would sell more in two days than we would sell in two months. They parked at the Station and a shuttle bus took them to the barbecue. They alligator wrestled, climbed greased poles, etc. The Conservation Club had sideshows.

The ox yoke was on the wall in the Monroe Station when we bought it in 1960.

Talk to Vince: George Hunter verifies the yoke was used on the oxen that pulled the dynamite carts when the Trial was built.

Indians were welcomed on the Collier Tamiami Trail Tours busses in thanks for their help in charting the path of the Trail. Some of them still live villages along the road.

OUR LIFE IN COLLIER COUNTY
January, 1929 through February, 1934
By Lillian Larkins Weaver

Monroe Station on the Tamiami Trail today is nothing like it was in 1929; it has been moved back, rebuilt, and is now quite a different looking place. It used to be "hunters headquarters," and we spent some very happy days there.

Why did we leave there and later, Everglades City, if we liked it so much? Someday I'm going to write a book about our life in Collier County! It might put us on "Easy Street," or maybe people would not believe it! Here's a bit of what it was like:

We moved to Monroe Station when Lois was only a month old, about February 14, 1929. Bill and Uncle Lem Duncan, a former sheriff in Southern Illinois for years and years, had already taken over the station. The man who Bill replaced had been killed on his motorcycle while on patrol, so I wasn't happy about him replacing a dead man! But after we got moved out there it wasn't so bad. The station had two rooms and two restrooms with a small storage room downstairs, and a bedroom, bath, living/dining room and small kitchen upstairs. The stairway was on the outside of the building.

It also boasted gas pump and oil drums. One driveway under roof was pebble rocked, and we'd close the drive and use it as a patio during hot summer days and little traffic. Bill, with Gwen's "help," who was around two or three years old, planted the big rubber tree that is still there today. We were very happy at Monroe ... a "hunter's heaven" ... deer and turkey all around us. We had our own Fairbanks Morse light plant, which pumped our water and furnished our lights by direct current. Our back yard was usually under water, and I shot many a ground rattler from our stair landing. The rattler would be sunning itself on a floating board or other object. We always kept a loaded gun upstairs and one downstairs. Many times I would start up or down the stairs and then have to go back to get the gun to kill a moccasin that was stretched across one of the lower steps.

Bill killed a deer one day and brought it to the pump house in back and dressed it. Then he put it in our icebox. That night or early in the morning we were awakened by a panther scream. We had been talking the day before about what we'd do if a hurricane came. The building was so tall and narrow that we were afraid to stay in it during a storm. The panther's scream sounded like the scream of the wind in a hurricane and we both sat straight up in bed and as I threw the covers off I said, "Let's get the kids and get out of here!" Then we were wide awake and everything was still and quiet. No sounds even of a car passing, so we asked aloud, "What WAS that?" Bill went downstairs and looked around but found nothing unusual. The next morning when he went down to open up the station he saw big panther tracks in front of the door and around the pump house. The water was low and it was just a bit muddy there to show its tracks clearly, that it had been lured there by the smell of the fresh-killed deer.

We ate wild venison, turkey and fish so much that beefsteak purchased at a store was a treat! You can understand then why Bill loved it there in such wilderness! I liked it though there were a lot of accidents and many dangerous things we had to take care of. I look back now and wonder how I ever went through what I did, but I didn't think much about it then. I can understand how my mother worried about me with Gwen and Lois just babies, without a telephone for a long time, only Indians nearby, and our nearest white neighbors were eight miles east.

We had a hurricane that fall of 1929. We went to Ochopee where we made new friends and everyone went to Bryant Janes' boarding house. The storm was not a bad one but did shake that big one story house more than was nice! The children slept through it and we adults stayed up all night. The station wasn't damaged much, a door screen torn loose. Deer had come out to the highway to get to dry ground, and some of the men killed them out of season!

At times at night Bill had to help Sheriff Louis Thorpe, and I was alone at the station with the two babies. I had some unpleasant experiences with drunks a few times and a great worry was Gwen who never saw a stranger! I feared someone would kidnap her. One woman, wanted to buy her said, "I'll give you a big price for her. She will have a good home and everything she wants!" I told her I didn't raise babies for sale! We really got all kinds of customers.

One time Bill had to go to Miami in late afternoon and spend the night with his dad because of some problem about exchanging motorcycles. He couldn't get the other one until the next morning. He told me to close the station before I had to turn on the lights and get the babies upstairs. Just as I had Lois upstairs in her crib and had already locked the pumps and was getting money out of the cash register as the last thing to do, Gwen and I saw a car drive up with five of the toughest looking men I'd ever seen from Ybor City (Tampa). I had to unlock the gas pump and give them gas and oil and they also bought drinks, cigars, etc. They were surprised that I, a woman, waited on them and no man around. I heard one say, "Hun! A woman!" and to me, "Where's your husband?" I tried to be calm and not show how scared I was and I lied with a poker face or tried to: "He is upstairs taking a bath." They milled around some inside and others outside talking amongst themselves. I went inside as soon as I had filled their gas tank and tried to keep Gwen behind the counter with me but she couldn't see over it and would run around so that she could see and talk to the men. Two or three more times I was asked about my husband, where he was, etc., and I kept to the same story, expanding upon it a bit by saying that he had been out in the woods with the sheriff looking for a moonshine still (which he often had) and had to bathe and change clothes. I knew that they were puzzled, doubting my words. Yet why would a woman be left alone so far from any other civilization? And if my husband was home, why did I have the pump locked and all but one door locked and it not yet dark? For all of the half-hour that they walked around and talked I stood behind the counter by the cash register where Bill's loaded .45 lay underneath on a shelf within reach of my hand. They finally left, and it didn't take me long to get locked up and upstairs, taking the cash and the .45 with me.

Seminole Indians, drunk and fighting amongst themselves scared me a time or two. Most of the Indians were fine. Captain Tony Tigertail lived not far away and came to visit frequently. The Indian squaws were delighted to see such a white baby and snow white hair, and I had to watch them or they would pick Lois up. They weren't very clean, you see.

Another time two drunk white men stopped just after Bill had left for Everglades City. One of them was from South Miami and I knew him… "sort of no account" … not bad, but lazy. They were in a Model A coupe and wanted to see Bill. I tried to get rid of them by telling them that they could catch him at Ochopee, but they wouldn't go. The other fellow that I didn't know kept bragging about being one of Al Capone's men! That coupe was a mess and so were their clothes. I took cokes out to them as I didn't want them to get out of their car, but once when I was getting the drinks the South Miami man got Gwen up in the car and on his lap! He was harmless, just talking to her. "She is his good friend Bill Weaver's little girl!" I finally got her out explaining that we didn't allow her to get into other people's cars for fear someone would kidnap her. A businessman happened to stop to put water in his radiator and I asked him to help me get rid of the drunks, but he said, "I haven't time to fool up with drunks!" He left but did stop at Red Weaver's station (no relation) the first station beyond Carnestown and told her that I had drunks on my hands and that my phone was out from the hurricane. Red called headquarters in Everglades City (D. Graham Copeland's office) Bill had just walked in the door with his report and he quickly came back. By then though the two drunks had decided to go on but they got only half a mile west of the station and stopped again, too drunk to go on. There is where Bill found them, took their car keys and hustled on to see about me. Then he took our car and went back and took the two men to jail. The "Al Capone" man was nasty and wouldn't walk or get out of his car. He was a big man, about 6'2" and very heavy, but Bill (5' 9 ½", 165 pounds) took him by the collar and belt and dragged him out of the car and down that rough road to his car, threw him on the floor using his foot to shove him on in. Then the man straightened up and sat up in the seat very indignantly. Bill didn't jail the South Miami man but brought him back with him to sleep it off. The next morning the other fellow was released and came out and they both apologized to me.

We spent a couple of months in Miami that winter of 1929 and 1930. Bill worked in Miami Beach, rode a motorcycle, but in January his Uncle Lem Duncan again came down from Illinois with his son this time and we moved back to Monroe where we stayed until January 1932. By that time the state had organized the State Highway Patrol and the Collier County Patrol or the Southwest Mounted Police as it was then called, was discontinued. We were running the station for ourselves and Bill was still a deputy sheriff at that time.

That Christmas of 1931 Chief Deputy and Jailer and also Chief of Police of Everglades City, Bill Hutto, was murdered by bootleggers he had caught down on the Point and was taking them to jail on Christmas Eve, riding the running board of a Model A Ford. One of them pulled Hutto's gun from his holster and shot him. He fell just south of the jail in front of an Indian camp there. Sheriff Thorpe called my Bill about it and asked him to stop and search all cars passing our station heading east. Bill kept the station lights on and flagged down every car. He had his shotgun besides a six shooter, a .45. I was afraid the murderer would shoot Bill down so I lay on the bed by the window upstairs with his 30-30 rifle aimed out the window! I'd lie down until I heard a car coming, then I'd get ready to shoot if they shot at Bill. But none did, although one car refused to stop and Bill let go a blast from his shotgun, aimed at the back of the car. But the car was going too fast and wasn't hit. The car stopped at the first station inside Collier County and its occupants were scared badly and they learned from the people there what was wrong and apologized. They thought they were about to be held up! We were up all night and the next morning, Christmas Day, the sheriff called Bill again to go to Immokalee to keep order at a big celebration there. It was while there that he stumbled onto the whereabouts of the murderer's car, so he was into the thick of the murder solving.

Sheriff Thorpe then appointed Bill as Chief Deputy, Jailer and Chief of Police, taking yet another dead man's place. We moved into Everglades City in January of 1932. The jail was housed in the downstairs of a two-story building, across the street from the Courthouse, which still stands today. Upstairs were the jailer's private quarters.

I agree that Everglades City was a pretty little town and seemingly very quiet, but it proved to be "hell" for me and all of us. I've often jokingly remarked that maybe I've a chance to go to heaven when I die as I've already spent a term in hell, meaning Everglades City! Collier owned the town and all but a very few people worked for the Collier Company (Manhattan Mercantile Co.). D Graham Copeland was manager and it was a little Hitler kingdom. Copeland dictated everything even the County Commission had to do just as he directed. Anyone who disobeyed his orders got fired, and he even dictated how we were to vote. Bill was put on duty 24 hours a day.

The bootleggers (it was during Prohibition) brought boatloads of liquor in very easily since the sheriff was in with them. When the sheriff knew a boatload of liquor was coming in he'd send Bill out of town on a trumped up call. It would be so far out that he knew Bill couldn't get back until the liquor was loaded into a boxcar and out of town. Thorpe knew Bill wouldn't play ball with him that way. Bill had a lot of friends in the border patrol and cooperated with all the Federal officers. The bootleggers who killed Hutto were local people and couldn't afford to go to jail. Thorpe knew who killed Hutto but to let it out would incriminate himself. Bill knew but couldn't prove this. The murderer and bootleggers would have liked to have gotten rid of Bill the same way that they did Hutto, but they had seen how he could handle a gun and were afraid to try it. I feared they would ambush him as he was out on the streets long after dark and there was a lot of high shrubbery along those streets. Not only the bootleggers who brought in their loads of liquor, but the alien runners were bad too. The smugglers would bring in Chinese to one of those uninhabited islands for a big sum of money promising to get them into the U.S. The poor Chinamen many times were left to starve, as the Federals were too close at the heels of the smugglers. They were more dangerous than the bootleggers.

Most of the women in the town were not the type that I wanted to associate with. The fishing in the Ten Thousand Islands is one of the best in the country and the charter boats made good money taking people out from other places, tourists, etc., but sometimes a group of townspeople would go out on a party. Certain wives would get their husbands drunk and out cold and then those women would have a great time with other men. I always wanted to go deep sea fishing but not on that kind of a party. Bill went out with just men several times. Someone had to stay at the jail, so both of us couldn't go at the same time, hence I never got to go, as I wouldn't go without him. I had three women friends who came to visit and we often played cards. My time was spent minding my two kids as the prison trusties did the cooking and cleaning for the jail, so it was practically like being in jail too! Many times Bill would be sent out by himself to take care of trouble at a tomato farm miles away at night, so I worried 'till he got back. Maybe he expected to be gone only an hour or so. Instead it would be four or five hours or all night!

Bootleggers would bring "shine" into the Negro quarters of DuPont and then things would happen and the sheriff would send Bill. So you can see why it was "hell" to me. Finally I said to Bill, "Let's get out of here!" And so we did in February of 1934 and moved back to South Miami. I've never had a desire to go back to THAT town although I did love it at Monroe Station.

Do you think anyone would believe my story?

POSTSCRIPT
"OUR LIFE IN COLLIER CO., 1929-34"
Lillian L. Weaver

My story, written in answer to my family's question, "Why did we leave Collier County?" which I was asked in 1970, was hastily written and now I realize that there were many things that we experienced which my relatives, especially my grandchildren, would enjoy reading, which I didn't have time to relate then. I now hope to do so for their sake, so that they may know more about their grandfather.

After surviving the '28 hurricane on Big Kraemer Island, we returned to South Miami and Bill was a policeman again. He also had some cards printed at that time to advertise his skills as a guide in the wilds of the Everglades. These cards were distributed throughout friends and family, many of which still exist today. Although he didn't make any money guiding hunters, he did go on many, many hunting trips, and was relied upon to find their way out! In smaller type than shown, the card reads:

W. "BILL" J. WEAVER
Responsible Guide of the Wilds
Actually Hunting of Wild Game a Specialty
Let "BILL" guide you on your Hunting Trip into the Wilds
Of Florida .. It will be a thrill you will never forget.
For Appointment Phone 4-9221, Dorn-Martin Drug Store,
SOUTH MIAMI, FLA.

MONROE STATION

What caused us to go to Collier County is an interesting coincidence. In December, 1928 one of the merchants in South Miami, Bruce Hayden, asked Bill to go fishing with him on the newly opened Tamiami Trail. The canal alongside of the highway was a good fishing place. As the two men were traveling in Bruce's Model A Ford pickup truck, about 15 miles inside of the Collier County line, the right front tire blew out and the truck headed toward the canal. On the way Bill opened the passenger door and climbed out onto the running board, planning to jump free before the truck sank. The truck came to a stop on its left side on a ledge of rock extending into the water. Bill found himself standing on the outside of the passenger door and out of the water. He looked down and saw Bruce sitting on the inside of the driver's door with his head just above the water. Bill helped Bruce out; neither was hurt. They caught a ride to Monroe Station, one of the Collier County "Southwest Mounted Police" stations, which was the nearest place for help. The officer there, Bill Erwin, called a wrecker to pull the truck from the canal and he also gave Bruce some dry clothes.

Bill had not known of the Collier County patrol until that incident happened, and was interested. He learned from Bill Erwin that it was hard for the Company to find competent men to patrol the highway, schools so far away and the women did not like being so far from civilization. No white people lived near, only Indians and animals for neighbors, and the traveling public was the only civilized people to be seen. Because Bill was an avid hunter and had hunted in that area before the Trail was built, he was very interested and immediately, after returning home, he sent in his application to D. Graham Copeland, who was Collier's manager of his Manhattan Mercantile Company, and practically ran Collier County with headquarters in Everglades City, the county seat of government.

Next, my daughter Lois was born on Tuesday morning, January 15, 1929, and Bill's uncle Lem Duncan of Carbondale, Illinois came for a visit, arriving the same day on the one o'clock train in Miami. He and Bill were planning a hunting trip into the Everglades as they had done several times before, but on Friday, January 18th, Bill got a message from Mr. Copeland to come and see him as there was an opening for a new patrolman. Bill and Uncle Lem went to see Mr. Copeland on Saturday, the 19th and learned that the officer, Bill Erwin, who had befriended Bill and Bruce, had been killed while riding his motorcycle on patrol on the Trail. So, instead of the hunting trip that they had planned, Bill and Uncle Lem took over Monroe Station the next Saturday, January 26th. My two babies and I moved to Monroe on February 14th.

Bill Erwin's motorcycle was badly damaged, so a new one had to be ordered and arrived two months after Bill and Uncle Lem took over Monroe, so he was there to help run the station until I got organized. Uncle Lem went home in March and when Bill began patrolling in April, I would get Lois downstairs in her crib or swing and take care of the customers and care for my babies on the days (every third day) that Bill was on patrol riding the Trail.

The gas pump was manually operated – the gas had to be pumped into the tank to the top then emptied through the hose into the car tank. Five gallons of gas sold for $1 and oil was $.15 a quart. Bill was paid $100 per month as a patrolman, and I was paid $50 per month for running the station. All the money from sales went to the Manhattan Mercantile Company. A man from the office came once a week to collect the money.

Shortly after we started operating Monroe Station there was a world championship prize fight held in Miami and for three days prior to the fight the eastbound traffic on the Trail was very heavy and many stopped at the station. People wanted to see the wild and beautiful country which the newly opened Tamiami Trail made possible, as well as seeing the fight. Our sales that week were $1,500, the highest we had during our tenure there. It was mostly for gas, oil and soda pop, sold at $.20 a gallon, $.15 a quart, and $.05 a bottle respectively!

All types of people traveled the Trail, famous officials and ordinary people alike. Many tourists were a bit afraid because it was so wild and beautiful what with alligators, snakes, panther, bears, wildcats, possums, raccoons, besides deer and turkey and the thousands upon thousands of birds flying in formation and roosting in the trees at night, all of which was scary to city dwellers!

Our most famous visitor while we were at Monroe stopped by just as Bill pulled in a big bass from the Loop Canal, west of the station near the bridge. A big limousine, driven by a chauffeur with two men in the back seat, stopped and the older an in the back called out to Bill, "That's a mighty fine fish you got there!" Bill went over with the fish and talked to him. Bill noticed that when he talked, the younger man tapped on the older man's knee and he'd stop when the older man replied to Bill. Bill said to the younger man, "He looks like Thomas Edison!" to which the older man laughed and said, "Yes, I'm Thomas Edison." He was stone deaf, of course, and the younger man tapped Bill's words in Morse code on Edison's knee. Edison was then living in his home in Ft. Myers. Little Gwen was then four years old and was with Bill and saw Edison, but I doubt that she remembers it.

Another afternoon, Gwen was with her Dad on the canal bank when Bill was fishing. Suddenly a young alligator rushed up the bank with its mouth opened toward Gwen! He didn't get her for Bill, as always, had a gun on him and shot the 'gator!

As I related in my first Collier story, I killed many snakes, some on the stairway so that I could either go up or down the stairs. One afternoon during the summer and there was very little traffic, Bill was patrolling or helping the sheriff in his work. Lois was asleep in her crib and Gwen and I were sitting in our "patio" driveway. Gwen was in her little rocker with her feet resting on an empty Coca-Cola box turned on its side, looking at a picture book. I was a few feet away, reading a magazine and she was between me and the doorway of the station. Out of the corner of my eye I saw a movement near Gwen and when I looked there was a small, about three-foot snake crawling under her rocker! I quickly slipped around Gwen and into the house and got the gun. When I came out the snake had gone into a stack of empty Coca-Cola bottles in the cases stacked by the corner of the building. It had crawled up through several cases and when it stuck its head out from between the bottles I shot it in the head. There it stayed until Bill came home and pulled it out. Bill often ran over snakes with his motorcycle – rattlesnakes as well as moccasins and others. He would be too close when the snake was visible to avoid hitting it, so he would lift his feet high as far as he could from the foot rests and then over the snake he'd go! He didn't give it a chance to bite him.

One time while on his patrol he saw seven buzzards sitting on one long tree limb which extended straight out from the tree trunk and at a slight angle to the highway. They were sitting side by side in a perfect line. He stopped and parked his motorcycle, then standing on the edge of the highway he took aim with his .38 special Colt revolver at the nearest bird and pulled the trigger. All seven buzzards fell to the ground dead! Bill was surprised and knowing it would be hard for others to believe it, he hurried home and took me in our car back to the scene to be a witness. All seven birds were lying in a row at the base of the tree killed by one bullet!

Buzzards had nearly hit him several times. One did hit his motorcycle as it flew up from the highway as he approached. They feasted on snakes and small animals that had been killed by cars. One day a Trailways bus made an emergency stop at Monroe. A buzzard had hit the windshield shattering it and landed in the driver's lap. A woman passenger, sitting behind the driver had been showered, too. Both driver and passenger had to clean themselves of feathers, filth and bugs. It wasn't pleasant, though it was laughed about.

Buzzards were not the only birds that Bill shot with his pistol. A number of turkeys we enjoyed eating were killed with his pistol. One morning in early hunting season we drove down the Loop road. I was driving with Gwen and Lois in the back seat and Bill beside me on the front seat. About a half mile from the station Bill saw a turkey still on its roost in a tree across the canal in the edge of the woods. I stopped and he stood at the edge of the road and shot the turkey with his .38 Special Colt and with one shot, the turkey fell to the ground. There was no bridge or boat to cross the canal, so Bill put his gun on the car seat and dove into the canal to swim across and get the turkey. When he dove in Gwen started screaming, "Daddy! Daddy!" She thought he would drown, but she calmed down when he climbed out on the either side, but started screaming again when he dove in with the turkey and swam back and didn't stop 'till he climbed out. She wasn't afraid of the gunshot. She loved to watch him shoot his pistol. When she was just a baby, just old enough for him to hold her with his left arm and her right arm on his shoulder, she would hold real still while he aimed his gun with his right hand at a target and when the gun would go off she would laugh and clap her hands, trying to jump up and down in his arms.

About every two weeks on a day Bill was not patrolling I would take Gwen and Lois to visit my mother and other relatives in South Miami and do a bit of shopping. Grandma was very special to Gwen and she looked forward to going to see her Grandma. One afternoon Gwen was riding her tricycle in the "front yard" which was the driveway next to the station, and during the summer and so little traffic we used it as a patio. Lois was asleep in her crib and Bill and I were busy and failed to keep an eye on Gwen for several minutes. When we noticed that she wasn't passing the doorway as she had been we went to check on her and we couldn't find her anywhere. What could have happened to her? We were searching and worried when a car stopped and the driver said to us, "There is a child riding a tricycle down the highway!" We stepped into the road and we could just see a tiny object moving along the side of the road. We were happy and thanked the man. Bill got in our car, caught up with her and asked, "Gwen, where are you going?" "I'm going to see my Grandma," she replied. Bill told her, "Let's go back home now and Mother will take you to see Grandma soon!" We didn't forget to keep check on her after that.

With Gwen three years old at the time and very active and Lois just a year old and walking, I had to have help with them, so we got a young woman from Kendall to take care of them, mainly Lois and Gwen was with me most of the time. During our three years on the trail we had four different helpers, the first three stayed only a few months and they needed or wanted to quit. The third year Bertha and her daughter, Mary Lee stayed with us and were there when we moved into Everglades City in January, 1932. Bertha then married Earl McGill and they took over the station when we left.

My brother Horace spent the summer of 1930 with us. He was a big help in running the station and good company. So good with Gwen and Lois, but he and Bill were buddies from the time they first met when Horace was only nine years old. He loved guns like Bill did, although he was not much for hunting. He loved to shoot at targets and do trick shooting, like tossing coins or other small objects into the air and shooting them. He and Bill were pretty well matched in target shooting. They tried all sorts of stunts. Because our backyard was usually under water I had a pulley-type clothesline attached at one end to a tall cypress tree and the other end to the house by the kitchen door. I kept my clothespins on one of the two lines so that they were handy whenever I hung up clothes on the other line. The pins would be pulled towards me as the clothes were pinned and pulled out. I had a time keeping pins on the line that summer because Bill and Horace found them to make good targets as they sharpened their shooting skills. Another stunt that they did was to use empty Coke bottles as "clay pigeons" like trap shooting. One would be on the west side of the house and the other on the east side. The one on the west would throw a bottle behind the house so that it would come flying into view of the one on the east side and he'd try to hit it. We had to make good on a lot of busted Coke bottles. That was a summer that I won't forget.

One stunt that Bill did that I saw him do but I never enjoyed, though he was asked to do it quite a number of times, just to show some visitor: At a garage in Ochopee, Alto Griffin, the owner, would give one of the Negro employees there a long cigar and he was happy to puff it until there was about a half inch of ashes on the end. Bill would then have him stand straight and still with the cigar straight out from his lips, and Bill would shoot the ashes off and the Negro would smile and enjoy his cigar. When he asked if he wasn't afraid to do that he would reply, "Naw. I knows he wouldn't hit me!"

One bright moonlight night we were shaken awake by something that hit the big metal "South West Mounted Police" sign which hung over and was attached to the station. We wondered what that could have been, and when Bill went down to check and got to the bottom of the stairway a big turkey gobbler flew off. We figured a panther had scared him off his roost and he was blinded by the moonlight shining on the metal sign, which he must have hit, so hard that it stunned him.

The trail was a fine fishing place, especially where the Loop Canal joined the Tamiami Canal. Many fishermen came on weekends and winter residents from Miami and Coral Gables area, would come during the week. One man who owned a summer camp on a lake in Wisconsin came often. He wore knickers and they seemed to have enormous pockets. When he got thirsty he'd come into the station for a cold drink and in trying to find his money he'd pull out several big bass before he could find his wallet.

One summer though was a poor fishing time. We had a long drought and the canals, usually 15 to 20 feet deep at center, got very low and was only about five feet that summer. Then we had a storm off the Gulf coast and we had a lot of rain which washed the silt (the dusty topsoil) from the swamps into the canals. The silt killed all the fish and the surface of the water was a solid mass of dead fish, which made a "lovely fragrance" for us at the station! The watershed where the water flow divided east and west was just three miles east of Monroe and it took about ten days for the slow current to take all the dead fish away as well as the awful stench! Since that summer it's hard for me to enjoy fish if I have to clean and cook them. Fishermen who left their shrimp bait on the bridge banister to spoil didn't help change my love of fish.

In my first Collier story I told about some incidents with Indians but there were a number that I did not tell about. Captain Tony Tigertail and his family lived not far from Monroe and he was a frequent visitor. Often two women came with him all dressed in their regular Indian clothes. Short, knee-length dresses for Captain Tony and the long, ankle-length dresses for the women with multiple strings of beads around their necks. Bill and Captain Tony were good friends. He'd greet Bill, "How Captain Bill?" If Bill was not there, Captain Tony would ask of me, "How Captain Bill?" I'd tell him that he was with the sheriff or elsewhere, as he couldn't speak but a few words of English his conversations were just words that gave us enough from which to understand what he meant. The women never tried to talk to us but loved to chatter about Gwen and Lois to each other. A lot of younger Indian men wore pants and shirts but the children wore Indian style clothes. I love to sew but I never would have had the patience to make those multicolored dresses which had designs formed by sewing together tiny pieces of cloth squares, triangles, rectangles and stripes so beautifully made. I never saw the Indian men bathing, but I suppose that they bathed in the canal like the women did, all fully clothed! The women never took their beads off but each year added another string. The older women had strings of beads around their necks from their chins down to half way across their shoulders. I wondered how they could bear the heavy weight.

There was almost no trouble with Indians except some of the younger men would get drunk. Bill was called several times to get drunk Indians off the highway. One time Bill found an Indian lying on the highway drunk not far from their camp. Bill asked another, but sober Indian to bring him a bucket of water. Bill poured the cold water on the Indian's head, into his ear. That water roused him up and he hollered something in Indian as he sat up and was mad! He saw Bill and pointed at him hollering, "White man, GO!"

Charlie and Billy Osceola, grandsons of Chief Osceola, had camps close by the Trail, but their brother Cory was educated and lived on the Oklahoma Indian Reservation. He visited his brothers often and wore white man's clothes and spoke good English. It was interesting when he and his brothers would come to Monroe because the station would smell like the woods!

There was one Indian that was an odd one and some said he was a "medicine man." He seemed to be a loner, couldn't speak a word of English and "talked" by actions. He came into the station one day and started looking over the counter at a shelf that held cans and bottles of patent medicine, foods, cigarettes, etc. for sale. I saw that he wanted something, so I began taking items off the shelf to show to him, but he'd shake his head and utter and sound that meant "no." I'd put it back only to take another item and he'd shake his head, "no." I'd taken at least a dozen items off and got a "no" response, so then he tilted his head back, made as if to pour some water in his mouth saying, "Oogle, oogle, oogle," then with same hand point downward from his butt, said, "Sht, sht, sht." I then took a package of Ex-Lax down from the shelf and he smiled, nodding his head, saying, "Uh, uh, uh!"

An unusual and rather embarrassing, though funny, incident happened one afternoon. Our pump house, housing the pump which pumped our water into a big tank above the house was joined to the back of the station. The eaves of the roof were just behind the window of the men's rest room. The pump was running when a car with two middle-aged couples stopped. All were nicely dressed and one of the men was wearing suspenders with dark trousers and white shirt. He went into the men's rest room and was there several minutes when the water tank overflowed and the water came pouring down on the pump house roof, just outside the window, which was directly behind and above the toilet tank. The water hitting the roof scared the man and evidently when he jumped up from the toilet seat his suspenders dropped into the commode and as he flipped the suspenders up to his shoulders they brought some of the contents of the commode with them, some splattered the ceiling and some on his white shirt. He came bolting out the door and on outside. He was scared and embarrassed! His wife and the other couple began laughing and kidding him. They told him that he'd have to ride outside of the car on the spare tire. (Spare tires were fastened to the back of cars then.) They asked me where was the closest place he could buy a new shirt. I told him that he "might" find one at Ochopee, but if not it would be Everglades City some twenty-one miles further on. We had a bit of a cleaning job to do!

While Bill was helping to pick up bodies after we survived the '28 hurricane on Lake Okeechobee, he met Doyle Carlton who was at that time a candidate for the governor of Florida and had come to survey the devastation that the storm had caused. Bill was dirty, barefoot and unshaven when they met and talked. About two years later at the beginning of hunting season Bill was in uniform and on patrol on the Trail one afternoon and stopped at a hunter's camp that was close by the highway to talk to them. The then Governor Carlton had just stopped there also to visit with his brother, one of the hunters. Governor Carlton recognized Bill, recalling where and when he first met him. It was quite a surprise to Bill that he would be recognized wearing such a different "uniform."

Their paths crossed once more, though sadly, nearly two years later when another hunting season opened and saw hunters in the woods along the Trail. One day Bill received a message from the sheriff that a hunter had been killed in the woods north of the Trail. Bill was asked to take a crew of jail trustees, machetes, a stretcher and a judge along to act as a coroner to meet a hunter who waited in Ochopee. A narrow footbridge was the only means of getting across the canal in that area as no vehicle could cross. The hunter who brought the message led the way to the scene of the accident, a distance of a mile or more north and through the woods. It was late in the afternoon when they arrived, and it was then that Bill learned that it was Governor Carlton's brother who was killed in a freak accident, shot by his brother-in-law. The brother-in-law had shot a deer with buckshot which killed the deer, but one of the buckshot ricocheted from a tree, flying to the side and back, striking the governor's brother in the eye, killing him instantly. There were two or three other men in the hunting party who witnessed the accident. It was dark before they got started on their way back to the Trail. There was no trail or pathway hewn out, so they had to cut their way through with machetes, winding a crooked path around the trees and heavy undergrowth, with Bill leading the way toward the Trail. He was a woodsman. He'd get lost traveling the highways in a car, but never in the woods! The coroner though, was lost and kept arguing with Bill that he was leading them toward Lake Okeechobee – due north! The other men had their hands full with the other brother-in-law who wanted and tried to kill himself by getting away and getting lost. About midnight Bill asked the still griping coroner, "What highway is there between the Trail and Lake Okeechobee that cars travel on, and do you see those headlights going east and west? What highway is it if it isn't Tamiami Trail?"

Soon after seeing those lights they came to the canal, emerging from the woods less than fifty feet from the footbridge, which they had crossed over earlier. The brother-in-law never got over the tragedy his gunshot had caused, and we learned sometime later that within a year he had committed suicide, causing more suffering for the family. Bill saved a sweet and gracious letter from Mrs. Carl S. Carlton of Wauchula, thanking him for his kindness and assistance he gave her and the family during the terrible ordeal.

Bill practiced all rules of safety with guns all his life and though he killed many a deer, never did he use a shotgun, always either a rifle or his pistol. He used a shotgun for ducks, quail and doves.

EVERGLADES CITY

After the bootleggers killed Hutto the Chief Deputy, Bill replaced him and we moved into the apartment over the jail in Everglades City. One of the inmates, a trustee, was the cook for the jail inmates as well as for us. Dave, as he was called, had been a chef at a local hotel restaurant and had been arrested for stealing thirty dollars in the spring of 1931. He was to be tried in court that fall but he was in the hospital when court was in session, so he remained in jail and was to be tried during the

March of '32 court session. He was a very good cook and with a couple of women trustees to help him and do the housecleaning for me, that first two and a half months there I had nothing to do but mind my kids and just watch that the jail keys were not taken by an unauthorized person.

I just had to do something, so I made clothes for the girls and myself, even started making a quilt which Mrs. Thorpe had interested me in doing. She was confined to her bed for several weeks due to a foot or leg problem, and to make the time go faster she made a beautiful quilt while propped up in bed. I had just got started and enjoying it when the March court session came and found Dave guilty. With a sentence of one year in the state pen at Raiford, Dave mysteriously disappeared and Lillian had to get up and cook breakfast for all the prisoners as well as for ourselves. I never finished the quilt, but years later gave it to a friend who did finish it.

In reconstructing Dave's mysterious disappearance as cook, he had a private cell which he was locked into only at night from the time he finished his work in the kitchen until he was unlocked to make breakfast. He had to wait a few days after being sentenced until the authorities could get him to Raiford. On the night just before he was to leave the sheriff sent Bill away to a disturbance of some sort at a far distant part of the county and Bill told him that Dave was not yet through in the kitchen and that he could not go until he locked him up. But the sheriff told him to go ahead and that he'd come over and lock up Dave himself. So Bill left, but the sheriff didn't come to lock Dave up and by the time Bill got home about midnight his cell door was open and Dave was nowhere to be seen. We later believed that Sheriff Thorpe planned his escape for there was never any searching done. He had already served almost a year in jail while awaiting trial. I suddenly noticed a special butcher knife of mine was missing which my niece, Virginia Baldwin's Grandfather Womeldorf had made and had given to me when Bill and I were getting needful things after losing all of our household furnishings in the '28 hurricane.

I had help for a while with the housecleaning by the women trustees, but continued as cook for everyone for the rest of our stay there. It is hard now to believe, but the county paid only $.03 a pound for the salt pork which we used to season the beans, one of the main foods which we gave to the prisoners.

One day during the housecleaning a woman trustee had opened the window screen that was beside the girls' bed, a double bed, and failed to fasten when she finished cleaning. The windowsill was level with the top of the bed which was against it and the wall. Later that afternoon the girls were playing on the bed and Lois began to kick the screen back and forth and was catching the screen with her foot to kick out again, but in her efforts, slipped out the open window and fell to the ground below just two stories down. We thought she happened to hit the seat of their swing and it might have broken her fall, but in later years she told me that no, she sat up from the ground, crawled to the swing and stood up, tried to climb up on its seat, but fell again, and that was when we found her. One of the white men prisoners saw her fall right beside his cell window which he had been looking out. He hollered something, which I didn't understand, but the trustee woman did, as did Gwen who came running to me saying that Lois had just fallen out of the window! Meanwhile, the prisoner's hollering had scared her too, Lois has told me. We rushed down the stairs fearing that she had been killed, and found her standing up with her hand on her hip in sort of a daze. It was an awful scare for us all and we were so thankful that the emergency examination showed she was not seriously hurt, but her back was sore for some time. She was taken to a chiropractor when we went to Miami the following week, and follow-up treatments were done after we left for an out of state trip and our girls were left with my sisters who got her to the doctor.

When we moved into our apartment over the jail we had more room for furniture and needed more. My brother Vance was a skilled carpenter and made many beautiful and useful things of wood. I have a treasure that he made for me soon after we moved to Everglades City, a solid cedar cabinet that is 38" wide, 19" deep and stands 62" high and is on rollers. It has three shelves, making four areas for storage and is closed by a double door latched at the center. When Vance and my brother

Pat brought it to me it could not be brought up the narrow stairway, so Vance took it apart and after getting the pieces up the stairs he put it back together upstairs. When we moved back to South

Miami in 1934 getting that cedar cabinet down into the truck with it full of linens was a problem. My brother Horace had come and along with his helper decided to lower it from the upstairs porch to the truck, but it had to go over a three-foot banister. I've yet to see something my brothers could not do! Emptied of the linens, the lighter cabinet was soon lowered to the truck and refilled with my things!

Bill was sent to the far corners of Collier County, Marco Island, Chokoloskee and others of the Ten Thousand Islands, and met some very fine men, old settlers like Ted Smallwood, Mr. Turner, Dick Sawyer, Mr. House and others, but those islands were a good hiding place for real criminals, hiding from the law and also the islands were an ideal place to bring in booze and illegal aliens! Bill helped the Border Patrol officers and they helped him in various ways. Now in 1990 and for nearly ten years past I understand that it is drugs that is brought in since liquor is legal. It is a drug runner's haven, and Everglades City is just a way station as the county seat was moved to Naples many years ago.

One of the worst experiences I had while at the apartment over the jail kept me awake all night. There were a number of big tomato farms off Highway 29 that runs north from Everglades City through Copeland, Deep Lake and Immokalee in Collier County. Usually two white men would oversee the farm and hired fifty to one hundred and fifty Negroes to do the work. The bootleggers or moonshiners knew when payday came, so they took their liquor into the Camps of the workers and when the Negroes got drunk there was trouble, often big trouble.

One night both Bill and the sheriff were called to go to one of the farms. They expected to be back before midnight, but midnight came and went and they hadn't returned. I never could go to sleep when Bill was out on a call at night until he returned. That night I went to bed but not to sleep, and about one o'clock I heard a car drive up, or rather I heard the door of the car close, and I heard footsteps come up the stairs and into the living room and the jangle of the jail keys when they were picked up from the cabinet where they were kept. I then listened for the jail door to be opened and shut after a prisoner was locked up, but instead the footsteps went out the door to the car and the car was driven away. I got up to check and watched from the upstairs porch where one could see all over the west and north sides of the city. I was quite puzzled. Why did the sheriff come get the keys, as I could tell it wasn't Bill by the footsteps? Why hadn't he locked anyone up? I watched the car go to the small hospital, stop for a moment then head north out of town. Where was Bill, I wondered. Did he get hurt and the sheriff brought him to the hospital? I wondered and worried the rest of the night --- no sleep. At daylight I started breakfast for the inmates but no Bill, no sheriff, yet. About 7:30 they arrived, put one Negro in jail and Bill came up and told a very relieved Lillian what had happened.

When they arrived at that farm there was one Negro quite drunk and was causing a lot of trouble. The whole camp was in an uproar. The two white men couldn't handle them, so Bill and Sheriff Thorpe got the one who started it in their car to bring him to jail. Bill was on one side of the car watching that the prisoner didn't get out or anyone bother him. Thorpe was on the other side of the car talking to the two white men. A lot of Negroes were standing around when all of a sudden there was a loud <u>bang</u>! And the sheriff hollered loudly. Bill saw a Negro run. Thinking the sheriff had been shot, Bill kept calling for him to stop, but he kept running. A Negro woman was scared and running also a bit to the side of the path that the man and Bill were running. When the man wouldn't stop Bill shot over his head warning him a couple of times, and the woman began screaming and fell down. Others thought that Bill had hit her or she thought that he was shooting at <u>her</u>. The man suddenly stopped and whirled around, acting as though he was going to shoot Bill. Then Bill shot him and wounded him, and he fell and didn't get up. When Bill got back to see how bad the sheriff was hurt he was glad to learn that he was okay. The big bang was made by the Negro throwing a pop bottle at the sheriff and instead of Thorpe, it hit the car close to Thorpe's head causing him to holler. It was the wounded man whom the sheriff brought to the hospital, leaving Bill at the farm to keep any more trouble from happening. Evidently Thorpe lost his calm and was confused and scared when he came to get the jail keys.

Bill had a very good mental filing cabinet. He could remember those prisoners' names and faces, recognizing them after years of no contact with them. He was good to the Negroes as long as they behaved themselves, and he knew how to manage one that didn't behave as he should!

Our life there was not all unpleasant. We had a number of visitors, many of whom were dear relatives. Uncle Lem Duncan and his son came again but he and Bill didn't go hunting. Bill's son, Frank, by a former marriage spent a couple of weeks with us. It was the first time that Frank and his two sisters had ever met. He was 18 years to Gwen's 5 and Lois' 3. Bill's sister, Ruby and family visited us and a number of my family just for short stays. Bill, on duty 24 hours a day and 7 days a week, couldn't spend much time with visitors, just when they could go out with him on his rounds, if possible.

Everglades City being "fisherman's haven," many famous people came to fish among those Ten Thousand Islands. One notable person of whom Bill was to spend some pleasant time with was the famous western novelist, Zane Grey. They would meet on the dock and have a wonderful visit.

I was able to go to Chokoloskee one night, the only time I was on a boat while we were there in Collier County. Sheriff Thorpe and Bill needed to check or get some information from a businessman on Chokoloskee Island, so they made it a pleasure trip for us wives.

One Saturday night there was to be a square dance in Immokalee and Bill was sent to help maintain order because sometimes things got out of hand. There'd be drinking and fighting. When he arrived he found a sad looking crowd standing around outside, so he asked them why their long faces. They replied, "We can't have a dance. The fiddler is drunk and can't play his fiddle!" Bill asked them if they had a second, an accompanist, and they replied, "Oh yes. The guitarist is fine, but without a fiddler we can't have a dance!" Bill asked for the fiddle and when they showed it to him he said, "All right. Give me the fiddle and I will play for you. But there is to be NO drinking and NO fighting or there will be no dancing!" Which is what he did, and they danced away as he played tune after tune from his early days of playing at barn dances, much to everyone's delight, and the square dance was a success with Law and Order saving the day.

Frog hunting was a night sport which some of the men enjoyed and Bill went with them one moonlit night. He took a cloth sack and a stick to hit them with and the group had good luck. Bill brought home a dozen or more and it was late when he came in and I was already asleep. He didn't tie the sack tight, just tossed it in the ice section of our icebox, which was on the porch, just outside of the kitchen door at the head of the stairs. When I opened the icebox the next morning to start breakfast there were live frogs all over the inside of the icebox. Imagine what fun I had catching those frogs and rekilling them! I had thought that he would kill them with the stick before bagging them, but he just stunned them and they came to in the icebox. Bill wanted frog legs for his dinner that day and although I dropped them in boiling water to be sure that they were dead before I skinned them, still though they were dead they croaked when I began pulling the skins off! Bill ate and enjoyed them, but Lillian didn't!

I was very thankful to leave Everglades City in 1934, although Bill continued to be active in some line of law work until we came to Ocala in 1946 and here in Marion County he worked with the police and sheriff departments, training on the pistol range or doing some gun work. He carried an inactive deputy sheriff card until about a year before he died in November 8, 1979.

Being a law officer's wife in those days wasn't an easy life. I told my daughters, "I want you to love the man you marry, but just don't fall in love with a policeman!"

The little town of Everglades was the seat of Collier County and engineering headquarters for the building of the Trail. The official opening was held with great fanfare and a County Fair on April 26, 1928. The anniversary is still celebrated here.

FURTHER READING

WEBSITES with historic documents and pictures:
>   Florida State Archives, www.floridamemory.com
>   Collier County Museum, www.colliermuseums.com
>   Reclaiming the Everglades, http://palm.fcla.edu/
>   Cemetery Search, www.findagrave.com

BOOKS with background and recorded interviews:
>   Carlin, Virginia, *I Remember Marco*
>   Perdichizzi, Elizabeth, *Island Voices*
>   Repko, Marya, *A Brief History of the Everglades City Area*
>   Tebeau, Charlton W., *Collier County; Florida's Last Frontier*
>   Tebeau, Charlton W., *Man in the Everglades*

PLACES TO VISIT with artifacts:
>   Collier-Seminole State Park (US-41 & CR-92)
>   Museum of the Everglades. Everglades City, FL
>   Collier County Museum, Naples, FL
>   Smallwood Store Museum, Chokoloskee, FL

Editor's Note: This and subsequent pages were added in the 2018 edition.

MARIA'S BOOKS

The End of the Oxcart Trail; the Story of the Roberts Family of Immokalee

The Caxambas Kid;
 The Life & Times of Famous Fishing Guide Preston Sawyer

Dwellers of Sawgrass and Sand, volume I

Dwellers of Sawgrass and Sand, volume II

Dwellers of Sawgrass and Sand, volume III

The Good Ole' Days in Naples and Collier County

Ochopee; The Story of the Smallest Post Office

Old Soldiers Have Nine Lives

Swamp Buggy Fever

The Tamiami Trail; A Collection of Stories

We Also Came; Black People in Collier County

Maria and her husband Peter in 1992 at the unveiling of the Tamiami Trail signs. Maria died in 2009 at age 86 in Naples where she had been given the Key to the City. Peter was devoted to Maria and published all her books but he passed away before her.

TIME LINE

1873 Barron Gift Collier born on March 23 in Memphis, TN

1873 James Franklin Jaudon born on October 19 in Waco, TX

1911 Collier bought island of Useppa, FL

1915 Jaudon began Tamiami Trail from Miami

1917 United States entered World War I

1919 United States passed 18th Amendment enabling Prohibition

1919 United States passed 19th Amendment enabling votes for women

1921 Collier bought Deep Lake citrus farm and surrounding land

1923 Collier County established by Florida legislature on May 8

1923 construction started on Tamiami Trail and town of Everglades

1925 John W. Martin elected Governor of Florida

1928 Tamiami Trail opening ceremony on April 26 in town of Everglades

1929 Great Depression started with stock market crash on October 29

1938 Jaudon died on February 22 in Miami

1939 Collier died on March 13 in New York City

1947 Everglades National Park opened on December 6 by President Truman

1950 Samuel Carnes Collier died during an automobile race at Watkins Glen, NY

1953 City of Everglades incorporated

1954 Miles Cowles Collier died from a virus infection in Palm Beach, FL

1959 Collier County referendum voted to move seat to East Naples

1960 Hurricane Donna struck the southwest coast of Florida

1968 McLeod Park established in Everglades City

1976 Barron Gift Collier, Jr., died from pneumonia in New Orleans, LA

1998 Museum of the Everglades opened

2016 Monroe Station burnt down

www.ingramcontent.com/pod-product-compliance
Lightning Source LLC
Chambersburg PA
CBHW060518300426
44112CB00017B/2725